RUNNING
TOWARD
MYSTERY

.
.
.

RANDOM HOUSE

NEW YORK

RUNNING TOWARD MYSTERY

The Adventure of an Unconventional Life

THE VENERABLE TENZIN PRIYADARSHI

AND ZARA HOUSHMAND

Published in the United States by Random House, an imprint
and division of Penguin Random House LLC, New York.

RANDOM HOUSE and the House colophon is a registered
trademark of Penguin Random House LLC.

Hardback ISBN 9781984819857
Ebook ISBN 9781984819864

Printed in Canada on acid-free paper

randomhousebooks.com

2 4 6 8 9 7 5 3 1

First Edition

Book design by Caroline Cunningham

To all sentient beings, who are the cause of profound *bodhicitta*;

To the teachers who have illuminated the path;

To my parents, who experienced renunciation;

To the Great Fourteenth, who is the North Star.

CONTENTS

•

•

•

PROLOGUE

. . .

The India where I was born, three decades after Independence, was a country struggling to navigate a path into modernity. It was a society where religion still played a crucial role from cradle to grave. My own family included both believers and nonbelievers, but every one of them was alarmed by the choice I made to leave behind a comfortable and privileged existence in pursuit of a contemplative life. But what they saw as running away, in defiance of all expectations that society had laid on me, I felt instead as running toward something that pulled me, mysteriously but irresistibly.

My decision to set out from home into something profoundly unknown sparked a long and painful discord with my family, but it also led to encounters both serendipitous and meaningful with individuals who helped to shape how I see the world. They were willing to engage with me, even as a child, because I came to them with an open heart and mind, and they became beacons to me, lighting my way. A journey that began by defying my family's expectations has also defied other predictable paths, crossing the boundaries of different traditions. The monastery where I live now and where I turn for moments of solitude is within the heart and mind; the whole world is my cloister.

Many of the events and individuals that I've encountered on this journey have been profoundly and inexplicably mysterious. The modern mind is ill at ease with uncanny events that defy rational explanation. We tend to look for psychological or cultural explanations, as if only what escapes those filters can truly be called mysterious. But not all experience fits into the binary categories of rational or irrational, and mystery is not merely what fails the test of reason. There is a realm of the mind where the experience of mystery is valid on its own terms. Understanding it may lie beyond the scope of language, but it is not outside the realm of human capacities. And sometimes, like a prism revealing the colors contained within a beam of white light, mystery serves as a portal to deeper questions and answers than our rational minds can perceive.

I believe that all humans are contemplative by nature; we all share the potential for contemplative exploration that beckoned to me. Whatever we think of religion, however we are culturally shaped, we are all drawn to deeper questions about the meaning and purpose of our lives. This capacity for embracing the mystery of what it means to be alive is available to all of us, our human birthright. We can choose to ignore it, but I would invite you instead to explore it.

Any reluctance we might feel at the doorway is likely rooted in fear, though our faintheartedness is not truly fear of the unknown. Our fear is more precisely the fear of abandoning the known, the comfort zone of the familiar, with its false sense of certainty and complacent promises. It is this self-created echo chamber that constrains our growth and makes the unknown territory of our deeper potential seem distantly strange and mysterious. The first step on a journey beyond these self-imposed borders is to hear the invitation that beckons from a place of mystery.

I was ten years old when this story begins.

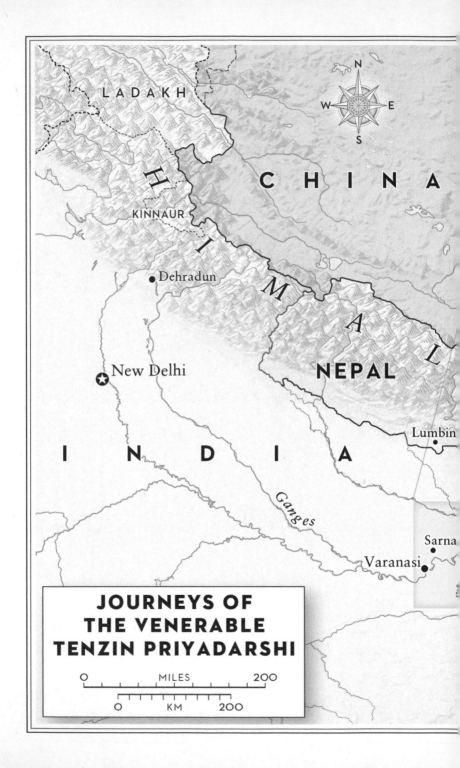

JOURNEYS OF
THE VENERABLE
TENZIN PRIYADARSHI

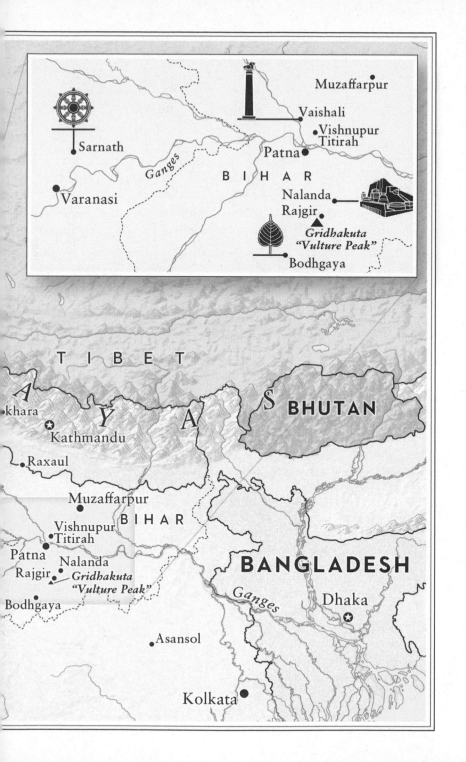

RUNNING
TOWARD
MYSTERY

.
.
.

CHAPTER 1

Going Forth: West Bengal, 1989

.
.
.

> It is no measure of health to be well adjusted to a
> profoundly sick society.
>
> —J. KRISHNAMURTI

It was two-thirty by the clock when I woke up in the semi-darkness of the dormitory, the dream still vivid and present. That man was back again, as familiar as an old friend. He had been visiting my dreams for four years now and still I had no idea who he was, where he had come from, or what he wanted from me. His eyes stared right at me with an open, forthright look, and his wide lips were pressed into what might or might not have been a smile. The expression was neutral—I couldn't say that he was happy or sad, friendly or not, but he was radiant, glowing with an intense energy. He was silent this time. He had only spoken once before, in a language I didn't understand.

The last time he appeared I wasn't even asleep. It was on the train just a few months earlier, when my family was moving, yet again, from Ahmadabad to Kolkata. Draw a line all the way across India at its widest and you can imagine how long a train trip that was. No kid could sleep the whole way, let alone one with my energy. I was in the top bunk, staring at the grimy ceiling and still perfectly conscious even as the metal rhythm was lulling me. Then out of nowhere, there he was. The dome of his shaved head was so vivid I could have reached out and touched the stubble. His eyes glimmered under fuzzy eyebrows that were as white as his crisp, white shirt. He wore a yellow cloth over it, fastened at one shoulder. It was all so intensely clear and bright, nothing sleepy about it at all.

I was six years old in 1985, when the dreams and visions had started. The very first time too, there was no question that I was wide awake. I was with a friend who lived in the same compound, at Evelyn Lodge, where our bungalow was. I had gone to his apartment to ask him to play and we were walking toward the cricket field when I saw what looked at first like streaks and patches of orange in the sky. Was it sunset already? That would mean it was time to go home, but it couldn't be. We hadn't even started playing. Then the colors resolved into shapes and their outlines became clear. Men in robes of that saffron sunset color, with shaved heads, were milling about. There was a deer and a small hut. Some of the men went into the hut and came out again. It was as vivid as if I were watching a scene from life.

"Do you see that?"

My friend followed my gaze, squinting into the sky. "See what?" He swung the bat at nothing. I pinched myself. That was what you were supposed to do if you thought you were dreaming. It made no difference. Slowly, as we continued to walk, the scene faded into the sky and disappeared. Later, when I got home, I told my parents, but they said I must have imagined it.

I worried that there was something wrong with my eyes. But I had no trouble seeing the blackboard in class, or the ball when it was my turn to bat, or the mangoes hanging in the orchard, waiting for my arrows. And if it was my mind that wasn't right? Well, it was right enough in all other departments. My grades were excellent.

And so it was forgotten, no big deal, and the memory would have been lost in the jumbled closet of a child's mind if I hadn't seen the other things later. There was a place that I dreamt of again and again, but even when I was awake it appeared very clearly to my mind's eye: A rocky peak loomed above a plain, wrapped in woods and scrub but with boulders and a cliff face exposed. I had a bird's-eye view, but I could see no buildings, no human mark on the landscape, nothing to hint at where this place was or why it should rouse in me a lingering sweetness, a yearning. It was as perplexing as the man who kept visiting my dreams, and just as persistent. There were other people who appeared at times, some with shaved heads and some with dreadlocks, wearing different shades of yellow, orange, or red. But he was the one I saw most clearly.

I was old enough to know that dreams, however weird they might seem, are normally rooted in the workings of our own minds and that waking hallucinations are not normal. I didn't have a theory—not even a half-baked hint—about what these intrusions in my mind might signify. They seemed to come from beyond me, beyond the world of logical sense, a genuine mystery that begged to be solved.

Now I lay there in the darkened room, listening to the random snuffles and snores of a hundred sleeping boys, and felt a mounting sense of urgency. I wasn't going to get any closer to the answer by lying here wide awake until the morning bell.

To find it, I needed to go out and search for it. After all, mysteries are how adventures begin.

It was time. I crept out of bed slowly. There was just enough shadowy light spilling over from the foyer to see by. Moving as quietly as possible, I put some clothes into a small daypack. I sat on the edge of the bed, so I didn't have to risk the noise of pulling out the desk chair, and wrote a note to my parents. Just a few words that revealed nothing so much as a ten-year-old's hubris—that I was leaving on a spiritual quest and didn't know where it would take me, but they shouldn't worry. I slid the note under the wooden lid of the desk.

I thought about stuffing the bed, but there was no point. This wasn't a prank. The staff would know soon enough that I was gone, and it seemed that a spiritual quest ought to begin with a certain dignity. I padded through the hostel dormitory, past the many beds with boys arranged in many ways, and then down the hallway. I put my sandals on and stepped out into the night.

St. Vincent's High and Technical School in Asansol was one of the oldest of the many schools that the Irish Christian Brothers had built in India, and the campus was vast. I kept to the shadows of the tree-lined paths, avoiding the few streetlights. By the time I had walked from the hostel to the gate, there was a hint of morning mist and the faintest wash of light in the sky. Dawn was still an hour away. I was surprised to find the gate ajar and no sign of the watchman who was usually there at all hours. No need for a story. A pedal rickshaw stood in front of the gate as if waiting for me. I climbed in and said, "Station," as if I were any traveler on a busy day, not eager for questions or conversation. He leaned into the cycle to start and we moved through the silence of the empty streets.

I knew these streets better than most who boarded at

school. My family had lived in Asansol before my father's job took us to Ahmadabad. Although Asansol is a huge industrial hub in West Bengal, where the British first mined Indian coal that fed the nearby steel mills and railways, its heart still felt like a small and sleepy colonial town. So provincial, in fact, that my mother was the first woman to learn to drive there. I was her passenger as she practiced maneuvering the oversized Ambassador around bicycles, rickshaws, and free-roaming cows, not to mention the pedestrians who would stop in the middle of the road to stare at a woman driver.

We were halfway to the station when it occurred to me I had no money to pay for the ride, or for a train ticket. I had the idea to stop at the home of a family friend who lived on Gorai Road on the way to the station. The man I called Bhola Uncle was from a zamindar family of wealthy landholders like my own, and one of very few friends in the business world who my father trusted. As a high-level career officer in the Indian Revenue Service, my father found his social life was much constrained by the fear of corruption. That threat of sticky social ties was also the reason for the constant reposting that came with his position and moved us so often from city to city.

But Bhola Uncle never leaned on my father for favors. Though his home was palatial in scale and the relatives who shared it with him flaunted their money in other ways, it was what he himself did with his wealth that impressed me as a child. Once a week, the poor of Asansol would line up at the entrance to his family's compound and he would sit at the gate, looking owlish in his huge glasses, and scoop rice or wheat out of sacks with a metal container, as an offering to anyone who came. He seasoned each measure of grain with a few kind words, very softly spoken, and a smile.

I asked the rickshaw wallah to wait. I crossed the lawns

and gardens of the compound, past the various apartments, guesthouses, and the relatives' mansions, and finally the big temple where I knew I would find Bhola Uncle up at this early hour, doing his morning prayers. He was surprised to see me.

"I need a hundred rupees." It was blunt but I didn't want to explain, just hoping that he wouldn't ask questions, trusting that he would trust me.

"So you have some expenses?" he said, with barely an eyebrow raised. I said yes. He reached into the pocket of his kurta and handed me a note.

Years later I had the chance to ask him what he was thinking that morning—just as my parents asked him soon after, when they were desperately searching for me. He told me what he had told them: "After all the years that I've prayed, all the good deeds that I've done in good faith, if the boy has stopped here first, my money won't lead him to trouble no matter where he is headed." I'm sure it gave my parents no comfort at that moment, but for me his simple response of a hundred-rupee note with no questions asked was an unspoken blessing on my journey.

Asansol Station is a big junction where several lines meet and many tons of freight move through every day. Even at that hour of the morning it was coming to life. People were stirring from sleep atop piles of luggage. A smoky mist hung over the platforms, the smell of diesel and damp coal and cooking fires. There was no line at the ticket counter.

"Where to?"

I couldn't name a city or station. I didn't know if I was headed north, south, east, or west. But there was a train already waiting at one of the platforms nearby and something about it felt right, so I pointed. "Wherever that one goes."

"Where to?" he insisted.

"The end of the line. Third class."

Though it wasn't scheduled to leave for another hour, the train was already crowded. An elderly gentleman sitting by a window caught my eye and gestured to the space next to him. I squeezed in. I wanted to avoid talking, but not be rude. Say as little as possible, let them think I was shy.

People and bags continued to find space that didn't exist before they found it. Eventually the wheels rolled. The windows had bars but no glass—a much clearer view, I was happy to discover, than the air-conditioned compartments in which my family normally traveled. The train yards gave way to mills and cuttings, and then to fields, paddy and jute, ricks and piles flashing between the trees that lined the rails, orchards of mangoes and lychees, and village after village after village. We made long, lingering stops that seemed to last hours in small stations, and equally long, unexplained stops in the middle of nowhere. Families unpacked tiffin lunches and passed me a portion as if I were one of their own kids. When they got off at their stop and another family replaced them, more boxes were opened, more snacks were passed. I wouldn't go hungry.

The day faded slowly and the constant wind turned chilly. I knew that in another part of the train there were sleeping cars where bunks were being spread with bedding, but here people slumped or curled where they sat. Heads rested on strangers' shoulders. I must have dozed off many times, but it seemed like much of the night I sat up awake, watching the small clusters of amber lights that we passed, glimpses of bare bulbs in village rooms, and long stretches of darkness between.

What on earth did I imagine a spiritual quest entailed? Where did that idea come from?

My family were Hindu, from a Brahmin clan who were landed farmers, rather than priests as one might expect. By personal inclination they ran the gamut from deeply religious to deeply rational atheists of Marxist bent. There was a rhythm of rituals that persisted regardless, whether the quiet daily habits of elderly women, or ceremonies that came around a couple of times a year and lasted for a day or two, enveloping all of us in the hum of chanted mantras and the clear, rapid dinging of the bell. Flowers and fruit and flames, red kumkum and yellow turmeric. Sometimes there was a meal offered to the whole village, with the kitchen ramped up to industrial scale. A year before, I had gone through the thread ceremony that marks a Brahmin male as an adult, and a few years before that I had submitted without complaint to the Mundan ritual where my head was shaved ceremonially for the first time. I was comfortable in the world of these rituals in a way that most kids were not. I was touched by the seriousness and, though I was notoriously rambunctious at most times, I was patient in these situations, sitting still as if on the shore of another world.

The spiritual meaning of the rituals seemed secondary; they were simply what we did. I had Muslim friends whose families had different customs, celebrated different holidays. Obviously the Irish Christian Brothers who managed our education had their own faith, which they shared in careful doses designed to pass as tradition and character-building rather than proselytizing.

None of this, as I understood it then, had any bearing on

why I was sitting on a train bound for an unknown destination.

When I was younger, I was fascinated by the sadhus who sometimes appeared in the village during religious festivals. I couldn't look away from the coils of matted hair that were wound around their heads like turbans made of snakes. One squatted at a small fire, coated with ash and dust as if he were a creature made of the parched earth itself, grounded in a way that we who wore shoes and clothes could only imagine. The pale ash painted on his face made his eyes all the more piercing in contrast. They held my gaze—eyes that were as naked as the rest of him, with a vulnerability transformed into unashamed assurance. Nothing to lose. Sometimes I saw sadhus on the train, roaming the aisles. They were allowed to ride free, without tickets, passing through our world but not of it.

I remembered how I would sit up in bed at night, eyes shut tight, willing my hair to grow into snakes by the power of my mind. Unsuccessfully. I had outgrown that silliness, though I hadn't overcome my fear of real snakes. And I was still more likely to approach a sadhu and attempt to strike up a conversation than to keep a safe distance and avoid eye contact, like most of my classmates would have done. But I didn't set out from St. Vincent's that night with a vision of becoming a sadhu.

·

The dawn spread a glow slowly across fields and orchards, and finally into the carriage. A mist rose off the damp earth, and here and there people were doing their morning business in the fields. Soon after sunrise, the passing villages each spread a bit farther until they began to blend together and concrete prevailed. We were in a dense city by the time the rhythm of the train finally slowed to a halt as the last batch of passengers rearranged themselves, gathering up bags and still-sleeping children. It was the end of the line.

I was surprised to recognize the station. Patna was the junction where we would be met by car and then drive a few hours farther to Vishnupur Titirah, the village where I was born and where we spent every summer. I had family here in Patna too. I could have gone to the pay phone. Within half an hour someone would have picked me up and the whole adventure would be over, as if I had gone in a circle and ended up where I started. But in truth that phone call didn't enter my mind. From the moment I had stepped out the door at the hostel, I never once thought of turning back.

It was clear however that I still had farther to travel. The din and crush of Patna at rush hour did not recommend it as a likely destination for a spiritual quest. I made my way through the whirlpool of traffic that circled in front of the station, and walked right past the Hanuman temple where I normally would have clamored to stop for *laddoo*. The sweets were unimportant now. I found the bus terminal. Once again, I was obliged to name a destination in order to pay the fare. Once again, I pointed at a nearby outbound bus and asked for a ticket to the end of the line.

That bus never reached its last stop. The driver made a valiant effort and pushed it farther, another stop and beyond that, long after the engine had begun moaning in pain. He took it slowly, alternately coaxing and cursing the last miles, then nursing it through the final throes with heroics on the transmission. The bus died with sudden silence on a stretch of highway that ran through rice fields. They were recently planted. Green shoots poked through a mirror of water that reflected the towering clouds of the late afternoon sky.

The passengers complained. The driver insisted that another bus would arrive to pick us up; we only had to wait. But the sun was moving lower in the sky and this wasn't a road that was safe at night. There were dacoits in the area. Passengers shouldered their bags, or balanced bundles on their heads. Many were close enough to home that they could hike the final distance. A passing Tempo stopped and left with a few more clinging to the back of the van. The bus driver smoked his last bidi and then stretched out on the back row of seats and dozed off. I climbed the ladder to the luggage rack on top of the bus and found a comfortable perch to watch the sunset. The light faded and I pulled a loose flap of tarpaulin over me to shield myself from the wind. The moon rose full, reflected in the rice fields. All night long it came and went, now bright, now dimmed behind clouds as the wind blew, and I drifted in and out of sleep.

It was still dark, with a stripe of deep sapphire low in the east, when I woke to the sound of passing cars. I grabbed my pack and hurried down the ladder in the bouncing headlight beams. A Jeep slowed down and I could see there were maybe twenty people jammed in or hanging off the back. A hand was extended. I grabbed it and squeezed between the hangers-on.

The Jeep disgorged us all at a bus station in a very small town that was not quite awake. This was indeed the end of the line. I started walking down the main street where the shops were still shuttered, the stalls boarded. I was hungry but not worried; something would show up. Within minutes, as I continued to walk, the town petered out behind me. I crossed a highway and I was on open road, fields to either side, birds loud in a dawn chorus. I walked for maybe an hour and still the sun hadn't risen, though the sky was bright to the east, on my left, where a ridge of hills stood in the not-too-far distance. More than hills, though not quite mountains, they rose higher the farther I walked. High enough to delay the sun that was incandescent in the sky now, just behind the peaks and silhouetting them. I stopped. My breath stopped, and a shiver passed through my body. This was the place I had seen so often.

A smaller road turned off toward the hills. It led to a small roundabout and the base of a chairlift, the metal seats dangling motionless like a carnival ride abandoned in the off-season. There was not a soul in sight. A wide paved path led up the hill. I started climbing. As I did, a deep sense of the familiar came over me. This view, the stretch of valley below, the rock face and the crevices in the boulders, the very shapes of the leaves that brushed the path—all this I knew. It wasn't just the recognition of the images I had dreamt. It was a memory of the place itself. This was my home, where I had once belonged.

And in the moment after that door of memory opened came a muddled flush of bewilderment. None of this made any sense at all. What was I doing here?

CHAPTER 2

Coming Home to Vulture Peak

.
.
.

Those who yearn to see me
with trust and noble intent
single-mindedly desiring to see the Buddha,
not hesitating even if it costs them their lives,
then I and the assembly of monks
appear together on Vulture Peak.

—LOTUS SUTRA, CHAPTER XVI

I kept hiking up the hill for what seemed like another hour, the day warming but still pleasant, the air clearer with each step I climbed. The path skirted the entrances to a couple of caves. I was about to explore when I noticed a wall, the edge of some structure half hidden by the peak above me. I continued upward. The path spiraled into stairs and then opened onto a spacious platform built into the mountaintop, surrounded on three sides by a low brick wall. In the center was a smaller enclosure, also framed by a ridge of brick. The space was empty; there was nothing to suggest how it was used. The weathered bricks might have been ancient. They reminded me of archaeological sites I had seen not far from our village, where brick foundations hinted at a rich and complex world that was now almost erased.

I'm describing what I saw, but it doesn't explain the unutterable sense of peace that I felt in this place. The receding hills framed the long view of the valley below, its business dwarfed to invisibility. The silence was vast. I felt suspended in the sky and yet sheltered by the slope of the neighboring peak and the rocks jutting behind me. After the strangeness of the journey, a safe harbor. As if the earth embraced me. I had been propelled here by something I didn't understand, but understanding it didn't matter. It was enough to have arrived.

I sat there for a long time, giving myself over to the calm. The sun was growing hot and sleepiness came over me. The two nights on the road were catching up with me. I decided to go back down to the caves to find a place to sleep. I had made up my mind that I would be staying here. I would be a hermit and this would be my home.

Back at the caves I found a sign, rusting and barely legible, in the bushes. The Indian Archaeological Society was informing me that these caves might be the stone houses seen by the Chinese pilgrim Hiuen Tsang on Gridhakuta Hill in the seventh century A.D. Such cryptic notes were a familiar feature of the landscape, and might have launched a lecture from any one of the historians in my family. But I didn't recognize the names and there was no one volunteering an explanation.

One of the caves was the very perfection of the idea of a cave: a smooth floor, a ceiling just high enough, a room just deep enough. I used my foot to scoot the dried cow dung out of my new home and sat on the ground. I leaned against the back wall and closed my eyes.

"Boy!" I jumped out of my skin at the shout. "What are

you doing here?" The words were barked with authority by a man with a rifle standing in my doorway, wearing the khakis and beret of the Indian Forest Service. As I came out, the sunlight blinded me for a moment. A second man stood nearby, also armed.

I explained that I would be staying in the cave, living a hermit's life. The first man told me that I was too young for that—though he spoke respectfully now, no doubt less in deference to my spiritual intentions than to the subtle markers of class and education that separated us. Besides, he said, there were snakes and wild animals in the area. There were even tigers not so long ago. It wasn't a good place to be alone. But I should visit the temple on the other peak, and he directed me to a fork in the path below us. From there a second path zigzagged up the larger mountain and met the landing of the chairlift I had seen earlier. The Forest Service had a post there, and the temple was above it.

Another twenty minutes' hike brought me to the site, and my first glimpse of a world unlike anything I had ever encountered. There was a huge white dome—a stupa, as I would learn—surrounded by terraces, with golden statues framed in arches on four sides. Beyond it was a smaller temple, also white. There are many buildings that one might casually describe as white, but in India it goes without saying that white is yellowed with age or streaked with the stains of bleeding concrete and spreading mold. This was a pristine, unblemished chalky white of stunning brightness, embellished with gleaming gold and bright yellow trim, that suggested unparalleled cleanliness, and a care in the maintenance of a physical place that was beyond anything I had ever seen.

As if in proof of this care, the only person I could find was a man busy cleaning. I tried to explain to him that I had been displaced from the cave, and was hoping to stay. He took measure of the situation and said I should talk to a person he called Baba, who was at another temple downstairs. "Downstairs" meant down the mountain, where I could get a horse cart to take me back into town to the hot springs. Then it would be a short walk from there. If I got lost I should ask for the Japanese temple. I was beginning to unravel from exhaustion and hunger, but as long as the next step was clear, I kept going.

At the entrance to the temple grounds was an imposing gateway where a small group of laborers sat on strike, chanting slogans half-heartedly. I couldn't decipher their demands from the words, but I hesitated. Crossing a picket line seemed sacrilege. One of the elders of my family, Basawon Sinha, was a father of India's labor movement. He worked alongside Jai Prakash Narayan (popularly known as J.P.) to found trade unions in the coal mines, railways, and sugar mills of Bihar. Basawon Sinha could make speeches for three or four hours at a stretch without losing the crowd's interest, and he transferred that skill to enthralling me and my cousins with his stories—of leaving school as a boy not much older than I was now to answer Gandhi's call to fight for India, of the years he spent in a British prison, with hunger strikes and a daring escape, of traveling in disguise through Afghanistan, which meant growing a beard and going to the mosque and praying five times a day . . .

"You didn't eat beef, did you?" I teased him with mock horror.

"Do you think I'm going to tell you all my secrets?"

He had passed away just a few months earlier, and though

his was a long life well-lived, I was sad that the stories had slipped away with him. Whatever the strike at the temple was about, I decided that he would have wanted me to find my own adventure, and not stop at the gate when it had hardly begun. In any case, the strikers didn't seem concerned whether I crossed or not. To them I was just a kid.

I entered into another version of that alien world I had glimpsed atop the mountain. The temple here was much larger but in a similar style, pristine white trimmed with yellow-gold, approached by a white marble staircase guarded by gold-painted lions. In front of the temple stood a huge stone monolith carved with Japanese characters in gold. They seemed far more complex than any other kind of writing I had ever seen, vibrating with an intense beauty. And again the cleanliness, the attention to detail.

I had seen countless Hindu temples, from the small shrines where Hanuman's red banner waved on a bamboo pole planted in holy basil in almost every village in the region to the teeming complexes that drew thousands of pilgrims on holy days. I'd visited several of the great temples with my family as part of the preparation for my thread ceremony, and found them disturbingly dirty. The filthy environment was not only unpleasant but felt wrong, as did the priests who would fold a request for money right into their mantras without even a pause for breath: *Om Kali, maha Kali, takadin, takadin* . . . I could do an imitation of their shameless begging that would make my sisters laugh.

In my own village there was a small temple dedicated to my family's lineage. It contained nothing more than seven small mounds of earthen clay. No statues, no painted images, no color at all other than smudges of red powder that people would rub on the mounds. One of those faceless lumps was called by the name of the goddess Bhu Devi, Mother Earth. Family and neighbors would come together in the morning to the well that my grandfather had dug right next to the temple. They would draw water to wash themselves, and then light a stick of incense and offer a prayer in the temple before going out to the fields or wherever their work took them.

So I had experienced, without giving it too much thought, a broad range of possibilities of what a temple might be or how the divine might be represented, from the humblest abstraction to the full Technicolor satin-and-sequins extravaganza. But there was nothing in my experience to compare to the very particular flavor of what surrounded me here. A calm intensity, an extremity of care, a mastery of detail. And holding it all like a heartbeat was the deep, booming sound of a drum beating a perfectly steady rhythm.

I followed the sound up the stairs and into the temple. The room was huge, a pillared hall of gleaming white, with an elaborate altar as high as the ceiling that glittered with gold. But my eyes were fixed on the drum, bigger than a barrel, which boomed to the rhythm of two polished batons in the hands of a man with a shaved head, wearing a white tunic and bright yellow robe. He was chanting along with the rhythm, but I couldn't make sense of the words at all.

I walked the length of the hall and opened the gate of the low wooden barrier that separated the drum and altar from the rest of the room. The drummer looked startled but he didn't stop beating until I sat down on the floor beside him. The sticks rested in his lap as he looked at me. *He must be Japanese,* I guessed.

"We've been expecting you," he said. He spoke in Hindi, very softly. His words startled me but they were of a piece with so much else that was profoundly strange that day. I didn't dare ask what he meant, whether for fear of breaking the spell or of seeming rude, or just the uncertainty of finding myself in a universe that worked by unknown rules. For all I knew, this was a routine greeting among such people. So I said simply, "I'm here."

"Have you eaten yet?" I shook my head. "Let me finish the prayers and then we'll eat." He raised the sticks and brought them down on the drum head, then began chanting steadily and forcefully with the rhythm. The sound vibrated through my bones.

While he continued, my eyes were drawn to the altar. A canopy of dangling gold ornaments hung above an array of statues, flowers, lamps, bells, and much else that filled the wall. In the middle of all this, dwarfed by the dazzling complexity that surrounded it but unmistakably at the very center, was a framed photograph. The elderly man staring out across the room was the one who had appeared to me so many times.

Yes, I had come to the right place. He was real, not a figment of my imagination. I could guess now that he was Japanese, though in the dreams and visions I had not recognized that he was foreign. In any case, I would surely meet him very soon now.

There was a small kitchen where the drummer, whose name I learned was Reverend Nabatame, made chai. We sat at a table just outside the kitchen and ate a breakfast of chai with chapatis and a little honey. By that time I was starving. Simple as it was, no meal has ever tasted quite so good.

I waited for Nabatame to say something, or ask a question, but he volunteered nothing in the way of conversation. I've never been shy. Even as a child I could talk easily with strangers: ask a farmer how the crops are doing, like a grown-up would. But it seemed wiser to follow Nabatame's example and say only what was necessary. So I said what felt urgent: "I would like to stay here."

"The laborers are on strike. If you stay, you will have to help me do the cleaning as well as the prayers."

"That's fine."

We ate quickly and nothing more was said. That would be the way all our meals were shared. Right after breakfast the cleaning started. Nabatame changed into a T-shirt and an orange robe that he wrapped like a skirt, and we got down on our hands and knees to clean the marble floors with a wet cloth. Eventually I learned that the laborers who normally did the cleaning were striking because they wanted their jobs made permanent, as government employees, but the temple didn't have authority to offer such jobs. Nabatame dealt with both the laborers and the convoluted bureaucracy with unshakeable calm. Meanwhile he was content to do the cleaning himself as long as necessary.

That floor was my challenge for many hours, many days. I had never done manual labor before. To be honest, I'd never had to do routine household chores either, as there were always servants to take care of such things at home. So there was an element of novelty in cleaning the floor, though it wore off long before the job was finished. It seemed the work would never end, and yet I enjoyed it. The perfection of the brilliant white marble offered its own pleasure, but even more, I was eager to belong here and to make myself useful. And I was spurred on by the photograph on the altar, excited with the anticipation of meeting this person. I kept a watch out for him, alert to the sound of footsteps on the stairs, a car pulling up to the gate. But he didn't appear all that day; few people came and went for that matter.

After a quick silent lunch of more chai, chapatis, and some

vegetables, we continued cleaning until it was time for prayers again. Nabatame changed into his robes and sat at the big drum. I sat beside him. He gave me a hand drum and I followed along with him. The rhythm was very simple; there was really nothing to learn. The chanting was also simple, just seven syllables repeated endlessly: *namu myoho renge kyo.* Nabatame made an effort to enunciate clearly until he was confident that I could say it correctly.

That was the sum total of the lessons offered. Nabatame didn't explain what the Japanese words meant, or what the purpose was for drumming or chanting. And I didn't ask. It wasn't that I felt intimidated. At school I was never shy to ask my teachers questions when my curiosity ran ahead of the lesson plan. At home, when the adults' conversation turned to history or politics, they welcomed questions. They were proud when you asked a good question, and if you didn't ask, they would frame the questions themselves that they thought you should be asking.

But I sensed that things were done differently here, and I trusted that explanations would come in their own good time. Or maybe I had to earn them? A spiritual quest would involve learning, but it would be a different kind of learning: not just information but learning that changed you. In the meantime, I was happy to sit beside the big drum and give myself over to the giant heartbeat and the vibration throughout my body. The endless repetition of the chanting and drumming seemed to echo the careful monotony of wiping the wet cloth over the marble floor. Perhaps something inside me would be very slowly polished, made to shine.

At one point Nabatame stopped the chant to recite a long text in Japanese, marking the rhythm by hitting a round wooden block carved like a fish, which made a piercing *tak-*

tak-tak sound. I just listened. This recitation also would become familiar with repetition over many days, until certain phrases jumped out from the jumble of sound. And sometimes we would sit still for a long time, and I understood that it was important not to wiggle or scratch or brush away a fly—not to move for any reason at all. But again, there were no explanations.

●

I slept that night in the guest room, deeply and soundly, until the drum boomed out in the darkness. I found my way back to the temple and sat down beside Nabatame. We chanted and drummed together for a couple of hours as dawn crept up and my marble floor glowed pink at first under the windows, with blue shadows, and then the pink and blue faded into white.

Over breakfast, I couldn't hold back any longer. "Where is that . . . person?" I hesitated because I didn't know what to call him, but even as I said it, it sounded rude.

"Which person?"

"In the photograph, on the altar."

"Ah. He is a monk. We call him Most Venerable Fujii Guruji, our dear teacher." He was correcting my rudeness gently, without a hint of scolding, in much the same tone as one might use to draw a young child's attention to some small wonder of nature.

"Where is he?" My question seemed to surprise him.

"He died four years ago." It was my turn to be surprised, and more than a little disappointed. But even though the news was confusing, something else was suddenly clear. *Bhikshu.* The Hindi word for monk that Nabatame had used to describe his teacher was vaguely familiar, but I couldn't have said exactly what it meant. And yet, now that I had a word for these people, my decision was made in almost the same moment. *Bhikshu.* That's what I wanted to be.

*

I had no awareness then of what a monk's life was, beyond the days that I shared with Nabatame. I knew nothing of rules or monastic community. My romantic notions of a spiritual quest might have been colored by comic book epics where rishis lived in caves and heroes disappeared into the forest for years to meditate so that the gods would grant them superhuman powers in battle. But I held no such fantastic illusions. I wasn't here to gain magical powers. And yet those stories held a kernel of truth, an urgent pulse inside an old metaphor that was leading me somewhere I had no choice but to follow.

I knew that part of the story was a sacrifice. I had to give up my ordinary life. As I swiped the damp cloth back and forth on the floor, I thought about what I was leaving behind—all that I had.

And I had everything. I had parents who were strict but loving and gave me far more credence than most kids got. I had sisters who were allies, seventy cousins—no lack of playmates—and grandparents who doted on me. I had orchards of mangoes and lychees and guavas that stretched to the horizon to play in, and in some remote calculus they actually belonged to me. I had Balram Bhaiya, the noblest of sidekicks, an employee in name, but in spirit my beloved elder brother. He knew every inch of our land, and which trees would ripen when. He could make a bow that was not just a toy, and arrows that flew straight, and he taught me how to shoot down mangoes from the trees. He was Drona to my Arjuna and our story ran from morning till night. He may have been the one who gave me my nickname—Khilari, the player, the sportsman. Always in motion. I was Priyadarshi at school and Priyadarshi was how Nabatame knew me, but at home I was Khilari, and when the old Ambassador pulled into Vishnupur Titirah, and I ran to kiss my grandparents' feet and then ran out looking for Balram Bhaiya, the shout would go up from house to house, "Khilari's in the village!"

But that was child's play and I had put it aside. The journey that had brought me to the temple at Rajgir was not make believe. I was learning silence and solitude, the skills of a recluse. Khilari was learning how to sit still.

I was eager to show Nabatame that I would be a good apprentice, that I was serious and hardworking, that he should let me stay. He was not one to reveal his feelings—he always looked stern but spoke gently when he spoke at all—but I sensed that I was a puzzle to him. He was used to dealing with Indian laborers and local businesses for the temple's practical needs, and sometimes young people would come to ask advice about studying or working in Japan. Most of the visitors to the temple were Japanese, whether tourists or pilgrims who were traveling to Buddhist holy places, or hippies hoping the temple might have a hostel. I didn't fit into any known category.

After lunch we would often take a break from the cleaning. Sometimes Nabatame had other business to take care of. Whenever there was time I took the opportunity to go "upstairs." A car might be headed up for some reason, and I would ask for a ride, or else find a horse cart. I didn't linger at the stupa or the small temple. The haven of peace on top of Gridhakuta—Vulture Peak—was where I wanted to be.

There was something special that drew me here, a serenity that was vibrant and charged, nothing sleepy about it. After hours of drumming and chanting, or the endless rhythm of polishing the floor, the stillness at the peak came as a jolt that wiped the senses clean and held the world suspended in clarity. I watched, barely breathing, as the slow shadow of a cloud drifted across the hills. A hawk rode the currents above the valley, almost motionless for long minutes. A thorn bush etched pale angles and edges over dusty ground, where an ant threaded its way through the sparse leaves of dry grass.

In the solitude there was a fullness. It wasn't lonely. On the contrary, I felt protected, embraced. There was company here even if I couldn't see them. When I learned from Nabatame that it was here on the peak that the Buddha, surrounded by listeners, first taught the sutra we were chanting day in and day out, the feeling made sense. There was something still powerfully alive here centuries later, echoes that the centuries hadn't erased.

Every time I returned to the peak, the feeling overwhelmed me again. I was home. I belonged here. I knew it with a certainty like the last piece of a puzzle clicking into place. This was where I felt complete, in a way that I had never felt anywhere else in my short life.

It was one such day, when I had come back from Vulture Peak to the temple downstairs and just started working on the floor again, that everything fell apart.

"Khilari!" a voice shouted. I froze where I knelt with the rag in my hand.

CHAPTER 3

Diksha: Passage into a New Life

·
·
·

Of the true Bodhisattvas,
The mother is the transcendence of wisdom,
The father is the skill in liberative technique;
The Leaders are born of such parents.
Their wife is the joy in the Dharma,
Love and compassion are their daughters,
The Dharma and the truth are their sons;
And their home is deep thought on the meaning
　of Emptiness.

—VIMALAKIRTI SUTRA

"We found you!" It was my uncle Vivekanand, my father's younger brother. The joy in his voice in that moment was overwhelming, but I didn't share it.

It was not chance that had brought him, of course. Inquiries had been made. My photograph had been fingered and held up to the light at temples all across the map, and probably mosques and Sufi shrines as well. If you were searching for a ten-year-old boy who had run away on a spiritual quest, where would you begin? My father's professional life in the revenue service could reach into every corner of Indian society. The extended family had means and connections, a foot in the halls of power in New Delhi and a grassroots network crisscrossing the cities and villages of Bihar. If I were alive, my father would find me, though it meant combing every inch of India methodically. Eventually somebody—I never learned who—put two and two together and made the phone call that my parents had been waiting for desperately.

My uncle Vivekanand was dispatched immediately as his home was several hours closer to Rajgir than my parents' home was in Kolkata. He arrived with a small entourage of distant relatives, accompanied by a Hindu swami wearing an orange turban and an expression of righteous displeasure. I didn't learn how they tracked me down until much later. At the time I was in no state to ask questions. I think my uncle had assumed that, once I was found, the drama would be concluded and I would simply come home with him. My refusal to leave the temple was not what he anticipated.

But Chacha-ji, as I called him, was resourceful. Like my father but even more so, he was equipped with a deep reservoir of emotion that flowed easily and voluminously. Though he was an academic and teacher by profession, the family tapped his considerable people skills whenever matchmaking was needed, and he took on such social tasks enthusiastically, roaring off on his motorcycle to visit relatives in the farther-flung villages of Bihar. He often brought me along for company and I shared many bumpy, dusty hours hanging on to him on the back of his Rajdoot.

Chacha-ji tried to pull an explanation out of me: Why had I left school? Had something bad happened there? Why hadn't I called home? I had no explanation that would satisfy, not that I could put into words. The only words I could find, the only thought I could hold, was that I could not, would not, leave. The very suggestion brought me to tears.

Nabatame took all this in without reacting. He calmly suggested that we sit down together to discuss the situation. I could hardly stop crying long enough to put two words together, but I sat with them at the table. "Why don't you come with us now?" my uncle cajoled me. "Your parents are not doing well. This has been very difficult for them. Your poor mother . . ." He shook his head. "You have no idea what you have done to her. Two whole weeks we've been searching for you. Two whole weeks!"

All I could say was, "I don't want to go home. I want to be a monk."

"Maybe this is not the right time," Nabatame said gently. "And, of course, you can't be ordained unless your parents agree. No one can become a monk without his parents' permission." This was a problem beyond my imagining, and I had no idea how much trouble his words portended.

At this point the Hindu swami jumped in. "You know, it is very curious. Why did he run to a Buddhist temple? Why not to a Hindu temple? After all, you are Brahmin, your family is Brahmin. This does not make sense at all."

My uncle gave the swami a look that could have stopped Kali in her tracks, and said to him calmly but irrevocably, "Shut up." Then he tried again, "Khilari, come with us now. Your parents have suffered too much. They are on their way to my house in Muzaffarpur. If we leave here now, we'll get home about the same time they arrive. You can talk to them and put their minds at rest, and then you can come back here afterwards."

"Do you promise?"

Chacha-ji nodded.

Nabatame asked the others to wait while we said goodbye prayers and he led me down to the room that had belonged to Fujii Guruji. It was an imposing space, gleaming white and dominated by an altar in the center. Framed photographs of Fujii Guruji in the company of dignitaries lined the walls. I blinked my tears back to see him standing next to Jawaharlal Nehru. I recognized the president of Sri Lanka and there were other vaguely familiar faces. And Gandhi, of course. Somehow this Japanese monk had not only flung out a rope that stretched all the way into a child's dreams and guided me to the mountaintop at Vulture Peak. He had traversed this other distance too, materializing in old newspaper clippings and the same type of musty photographs I had seen so often populated by my own grandparents, uncles, and aunties who stood proudly beside these same elder statesmen. It seemed almost as strange an accomplishment as appearing in my dreams.

It wasn't magic. At least some part of what I had discovered here was history, though I couldn't begin to guess at the how and why. In my family, history held a status that others might reserve for science: It explained almost everything.

The air in the room held a distinct smell of incense—not the familiar flowery perfume I knew well, but a more subtle and rarified scent, a calm breath of forest and clouds. "Can't I stay here?" I sniffled. "I don't want to go home. I want to be a monk."

Nabatame looked at me steadily, and then said more than he had in the whole two weeks before. "Maybe it would be wise to go. Being a good son, a good student—that's also good Dharma." He told me that I didn't have to stop practicing just because I went home. There was another temple that Fujii Guruji had founded in Kolkata, where my parents lived.

And he told me that if I really wanted to be a monk, he could give me novice vows now and I could be fully ordained later. I shouldn't wear robes or shave my head, he said, if my parents didn't agree. He was aware that in Hindu custom shaving one's head signified that one's parents or a close family member has died, and he could guess from Chacha-ji's dramatic arrival that my family would not be happy if I were to come home in robes with a shaved head.

Then he explained the vows that he would give me as a novice, or *sramanera*. They were a set of precepts of which the first and most important was ahimsa—to abstain from killing or harming living beings. It was why Fujii Guruji had thrown himself into the work of ending war, walking the world as a witness and calling out the prayer we had been chanting, and it was why he and Gandhi had connected. The next precepts were not to steal or take anything that wasn't freely given, not to lie or use words to cause harm, to abstain from sexual misconduct, and to avoid intoxication. And there were more precepts that would help to live a simple, serious life and protect my mind from distraction. He said the words in Japanese and I repeated them after him, step by step. Then he took a pair of scissors and snipped off a tuft of my hair. That would have to stand in for shaving my head. Finally, he concluded our ceremony by giving me a small golden statue of the Buddha.

I learned later that Fujii Guruji's order didn't normally give novice vows separately from full ordination, but instead did a single ceremony for a lifetime commitment. Nabatame had spent time in Burma before coming to India, and was familiar with the older Theravada school that held closely to the elaborate rules for monastic life—over two hundred of them—that were prescribed by the Buddha himself. In Burma the rules were still central to religious life and renewed daily in a way that most Japanese schools of Buddhism had abandoned since the Meiji period, though Fujii Guruji tried to steer his own followers by a stricter discipline. In Burma, a boy would be ordained first as a *sramanera,* and full ordination would follow at the age of twenty. Even the novice ordination was only undertaken after a substantial period of preparation.

It could be said that Nabatame was responding with a certain creative agility when he gave vows that he had learned in the Theravada tradition, expressed in Japanese, to an Indian boy in the bamboo grove where the first monastic community had lived together during the Buddha's lifetime. And though our ceremony was impromptu, it lacked nothing in gravitas and was a genuine *diksha* that changed everything. Nabatame offered the vows sincerely and genuinely, and I accepted them with the understanding that my life was now deeply transformed.

In a child's vision of what a spiritual quest might be, I had pictured myself as a hermit in a cave. I had not imagined how a life engaged with other human beings could be as spiritually rewarding as anything a hermit might do alone in a cave, nor how the young, green shoots of the spirit could be tended and nurtured by the company of others who shared the same dreams. It's true that the Japanese temple at Rajgir was tiny compared with the great monasteries that historically had many hundreds of monks in residence, though there were times when its own numbers swelled. I couldn't put it into words yet, but somehow Nabatame's presence in my life stood in for all of this. He was a friend, protector, and guide. A community—sangha—of one.

When our small ceremony was done, I understood that I had just made a commitment that encompassed my whole life, and I would live up to it even if the outer appearances were missing for the time being. It didn't matter that I had no robes. That small snip of the scissors had as good as shaved my head—just ever so discreetly so my parents wouldn't be upset.

There was one more thing I needed though. "Please, Nabatame-shounin, can I have . . ." And here the tears returned in force and I struggled to get the words out. "Can I have a drum? A small drum to beat?" He left the room without saying anything and came back a minute later with a package wrapped in a yellow cloth bag. He unwrapped a small hand drum decorated with beautiful Japanese calligraphy.

"You hang on to this for now. This drum is very special to me," he said, without elaborating. Then he looked at me and he said, "Your *samskara* is very strong." The word, as it's used colloquially in Hindi, refers to old habits of mind—older than this lifetime—that linger as deep memories guiding us toward good, like a wheel rubbing tracks in the road will guide another wheel that follows it, making it easier to keep to a straight path.

It was time to go. We said goodbye and Nabatame offered a last reassurance as I climbed into the car. "Don't worry," he said. "The Buddhas brought you here, the Buddhas will take care of you."

•

For several long hours Chacha-ji threaded his way through country traffic, muttering at potholes and bullock carts. He tried at intervals to chip away at my sullen silence. I refused to be enticed by sweet snacks posed as dilemmas: Should we stop here for the immediate gratification of *khaja*, or wait till we get to Harnaut where the *balushahi* could not be beat? I didn't want to be disrespectful, but I felt like he was talking to a child that I no longer was. I knew he didn't mean to be disrespectful either, but the sticky, golden towers on the roadside stall were no consolation for this feeling of painful disorientation, of being torn out by the roots from the place I belonged. I felt angry and that in itself felt confusing.

When we finally pulled into the driveway of my uncle's home in Muzaffarpur, the long fuse of tense silence ended in an explosion of chaos. On all sides, questions and accusations flew, tears flowed—not mine now but everyone else's. Where did all these people come from? My father's sisters were out in force, all five of them in my face. The crowd swept me into the house on waves of joy, concern, relief, and the kind of anger, loud in release, that means: You're safe! At the still eye of the storm, set apart by a white-hot aura of shock and sadness: my parents. My father turned away and disappeared without a word, protecting himself and me from what he couldn't control. My mother deflected her own pain furiously: "Were you trying to kill him? Did you even think what you were doing to his heart?"

In the cracks between the concern and the endless questions—the where, when, how, and most of all the why— I caught glimpses of the wild conjecture that had roiled in the wake of my travels. Kidnapping was a terribly reasonable fear. Any runaway child would have been vulnerable, and all the more so coming from a family that could afford a serious ransom. When no ransom was demanded, did that mean that the thugs had panicked? Left me dead in a ditch? Or that I'd been sold off to labor in some dark underbelly of what-worse-could-you-imagine? When finally I was tracked to the temple of a small Japanese Buddhist school at Rajgir, and the facts, as undeniable as they were odd, were relayed back to my distraught parents and the many relatives who had offered support and advice through every twist of the drama—that I had been discovered, swabbing the temple floor on my hands and knees—then the questions zeroed in on my motives as the perpetrator of this cruel torture of my parents. What on earth was I thinking? What delusion might lead me to abandon a loving family, a secure future, every possible advantage, and run off after religion like some poor, illiterate soul who had no better choice in life than to become a beggar?

My father reappeared, all ice and fire. He demanded to know whether something had happened at school to upset me. The Brothers at St. Vincent's would answer for this—if not for some abuse that had driven me out, then for the gross negligence that had failed to keep me in. My mother lamented that she had ever given in—not willingly, not happily, she reminded me—when I had lobbied to go there as a boarder. Her resistance and tears seemed excessive to me at the time. All I wanted was to return to the school I'd enjoyed when we lived in Asansol, a school that I knew well, instead of starting all over somewhere new when we moved to Kolkata. At least no one could argue with St. Vincent's reputation: It was one of the best in India, and so my mother had allowed herself to be overruled in the end. Because education was everything.

The two weeks I went missing were traumatic for my mother in ways I couldn't imagine as a child. While my father had thrown himself into the search as if he were leading a military campaign, keeping his worst fears at bay with tireless action, my mother had descended into a darker world. When my father's efforts failed to produce immediate results, she turned, in desperation, to magic. Clairvoyants and tantric seers are a dime a dozen in Kolkata, but she traveled back and forth across Bengal in search of those with stellar reputations, determined to find some clue, some hint of hope. Instead of hope they fed her worst fears. They claimed to see me wandering in a dim world unchained from this body, or they saw no trace of me at all, no signal from either side of the border between life and death. But neither their hocus-pocus nor the terror that was driving her were a match for her deeper instincts. She knew beyond hope or fear that I was alive and she would find me.

I didn't know all this until much later; it was years before she told me what she had gone through in that time. And yet, that day in Muzaffarpur the emotional information was all there, complete in its depths if unregistered except in the wordless place that mothers and sons share, even when they don't share.

•

At some point the interrogation became overwhelming. They were coming at me one by one, taking turns to press, as if each had some special claim to my confidence. But they asked all the same questions, over and over. Midstream of my aunt Meena's words I turned and walked out of the room, found my way upstairs and out onto the terrace, desperate for air. Even the view felt claustrophobic.

Normally, other people's tears move me instantly. They do now and they did as a child. But that day, the tearful drama left me cold. It was just theatre, an illusion behind a glass wall. I was ready to walk out at intermission. I wanted to go home. I wanted desperately to go home. And home was at Vulture Peak.

The door opened behind me. I knew without turning around that it was my father. "You can't just quit school, Khilari. If you don't get an education, you will be polishing shoes on the street. Is that how you're going to use your intelligence? Is that what you want to do with your life?" I didn't answer. "I heard you were cleaning floors in the temple."

"You don't know anything about cleaning floors!" It came out louder than I intended. I was angry but ashamed too. Screaming at my own father. He left me trembling, then came back out again a few minutes later, calmer.

He stood beside me at the balustrade and said quietly, "You know I can't tell you what to believe. Religion is a matter for your own heart, and I can't decide that for you. But you also have responsibilities to your family." He didn't need to spell out what those responsibilities were. The map had been drawn the day I was born. Only son of the eldest son. Brahmin. Like my father, protector and provider. A family that made history and then wrote the history books.

"I'm tired of answering the same questions over and over."

"You can talk to them all together. You can explain to them what you want to do, and ask for their blessing. If the family gives you permission, I won't stand in your way."

I stayed out on the terrace for a long time after he went in. The night fell heavy and humid under a layer of cloud that hid the stars. There was no moon at all that night.

CHAPTER 4

Trial by Family

·
·
·

Our firmest convictions are apt to be the most
suspect; they mark our limitations and our
bounds. Life is a petty thing unless it is moved by
the indomitable urge to extend its boundaries.

—JOSE ORTEGA Y GASSET

The next day, I went to trial. My father had managed to
gather some seventy-six members of our extended family.
They milled in the courtyard as if it were a festival day, sharing gossip—not least about the chain of events that had
brought them there. They crowded into the large sitting room
of Chacha-ji's home, with the overflow spilling out onto the
front porch. My aunts had the honor of the few chairs, but
most people sat jammed together on the floor.

I sat on a daybed at one end of the room, facing the crowd.
I had no idea what I could say that might convince them; I
only knew that no one was eager to be convinced. Most of the
faces were familiar to me in some degree. My father had arranged for carloads to come from our home village of Vishnu-

pur Titirah, a couple of hours away, and other relatives scattered around Patna had been recruited.

It occured to me, looking back, that this was a much smaller crowd than had come to witness my thread ceremony, and certain faces—those elders who were most respected—were conspicuously absent. I don't doubt that my father was ashamed of what I had done and anxious to limit the damage. If the whole sorry affair could be concluded quickly—if I failed to make my case to the satisfaction of the crowd and were defeated here today, if I backed down and gave up this regrettable fixation with becoming a monk—then it might also be quickly forgotten. Or if remembered, then as a passing phase of a commendably thoughtful and independent-minded child. One day this would be just another colorful story from my youth. And in his wisdom my father had arranged matters in such a way that a ten-year-old boy was both granted a sense of agency and obliged to account for himself as an adult member of his community.

For two hours they grilled me. They took turns. They took tea breaks, then came back refreshed, ready for more. The questions began simply enough, without hasty antagonism. Why had I run away from school? What had provoked me?

I spoke carefully. I told them I had no complaint against anyone. No one at school, or anywhere else, had mistreated me. Leaving was my own decision, made freely and not forced by external events.

There were a few taunts—"Maybe you would rather play than go to school? Maybe you can't be bothered to study?"— but I wasn't ruffled. That was how they talked to kids normally. Children were given a hard time to keep them on track. Everyone knew that I was one of the top students.

Then to the heart of the matter: "Why do you want to go back to Rajgir?"

"Why do you want to become a monk? What does that mean?"

Language faltered. Whatever it was I had found in Rajgir, the experience didn't come packaged with a lot of words. I couldn't begin to tell them what it was like, and in any case that wasn't what they were asking. What they were asking, really, was whether I understood the outrageous price that was attached to what I wanted, and that the burden of that cost would not be mine alone, but would be shared by the whole family.

"Nobody is saying you should not be a spiritual person. But why all-or-nothing? Full-time religion is what people do when they have no education, no prospects, no other way to survive."

"What is this monk business but escaping from your responsibilities?"

"Who will marry your sisters if their brother has shamed the family like this? Did you think that this is just about you?"

"Who would want a crazy fakir for a brother-in-law? Because if you do this to your family, for sure you are crazy!"

"Will you go begging? You, with your father in the finance ministry?"

So many of the questions were rhetorical and no one was waiting for an answer before firing the next shot, but the answer to that one came instantly. "There's no harm in begging," I said. "Buddha came from a royal family and he begged." The words seemed to come from someplace outside of me. I didn't know the story of Buddha's life. Nor had I ever seen Nabatame begging.

Then the mocking began in earnest. "You don't need to beg. We can sell that Buddha statue of yours! It must be pure gold, no?" There are ways to sting a child that only a feisty auntie knows. "Why don't you give me your yellow bag? It's perfect for shopping for vegetables!" At any other time, she would have riled me, as she often did, but in that moment I was impervious. Nothing any actor in this drama said could shake my calm.

I saw my mother standing still for a brief moment at the back of the room. She hadn't sat down. Even in my uncle's home, she was in some sense the host today and people had to be made comfortable. But the exchange about begging had halted her and the pain written on her face mirrored an image that was buried in my memory.

During the several days of celebration and ritual at my thread ceremony, there was one morning when we had to go out begging. My cousin Apoorva, Chacha-ji's son, had his initiation at the same time as mine, and we did the whole business together. Our heads were shaved, we were wrapped in the yellow cloth of a sannyasi, given a bag to carry, and sent out into the village to beg from each house. But first we had to beg from our mothers, seated with the aunties in the drawing room. Everyone was dressed in their party best, all shimmering silk and jewelry. When I held out my hand and asked for alms, *"Ma, bhiksham dehi,"* my mother surprised me by bursting into tears. This wasn't in the script. As if it were contagious, my aunts wiped their eyes and sniffled sympathetically. I wanted to say that it was okay, we were just pretending, but surely she knew that. How do you console someone who's hurting for no reason? "I won't be like this forever, Ma," I told her. But then with the party and the presents—new roller skates!—and the physically exhausting exercise of bending down a few hundred times to touch my elders' feet, I had forgotten that moment.

And now it was as if some terrible mistake had been made. Somewhere in the universe wires were crossed and shorted out. Because the whole point of the ritual of a small boy going out begging as an ascetic was that it was over and done with. That stage of life was complete and would not need to be repeated.

The arguments kept circling back to the dark consequences of abandoning my education. I would end up shining shoes or cleaning toilets, they warned. I would lose everyone's respect. "I don't want people's respect," I insisted. "I'm not doing this to gain respect."

Education was the true religion in my family, and quitting school the unforgivable sin. Whether they were devout Hindus or atheists devoted to the ideal of a secular India, every member of my family shared an unshakeable faith in the transformative power of education. We belonged to the Bhumihar class of Brahmins who traditionally were not priests but landowners, wealthy farmers who didn't need to get their own hands dirty and likewise didn't need education to get ahead. But somehow my family had become fervent converts.

Though my father's parents had no formal education, they made sure that every one of their children, including the five girls, was well educated; and they supported anyone in the village who wanted to study but couldn't afford it. We all knew the story of the girl who came running into my grandfather's house because her parents wanted to take her out of school to marry her off, and how he stood there on the porch in his white dhoti-kurta, brandishing his bamboo lathi and yelling at the crowd, "She is my daughter now! If you dare to come after her, I will break your leg!" She not only got to finish school but went to college as well. My father continued the tradition and, though his job took him all over the country, there was always someone from the village living with us while they attended college, and many more whose tuition he paid.

My mother's family was no less committed to the cause. Her mother was the first in her own village to get a college education, then came home and started the first girls' school. A portion of my summers were spent in that school, because too much vacation was not a good thing. We sat on jute sacks, writing out problems on graphite slates with lumps of limestone for chalk, but the mood was as lively, as warm and supportive, as the facilities were basic.

They all credited education for lifting people out of poverty, but my family didn't come from poverty. We inherited the benefits of ancient feudal power structures, and education had the salutary effect of opening minds and turning that world upside down. One of my mother's uncles was a leader of the labor movement and the Socialist Party; another was the preeminent Indian historian of his generation, with a hundred-some books to his name, and countless academic honors. His wife was the principal of the teachers' training college in Patna. My father's father had walked with Gandhi when he came to Bihar to unite the indigo workers, and his young wife—my grandmother—had struggled to keep up. "That guy could walk fast!" she marveled. His cousin, Baikuntha Shukla, was a martyred hero of the independence movement, hanged by the British at the age of twenty-eight—but before that he was a schoolteacher.

So when my relatives challenged me—"Why be a monk when you could be a sahib, a politician, a professor? Why this monk-punk nonsense when you could be respected and make a difference in the world?"—it was not blue-sky, dream-big advice to a child. There were genuine, real-life role models who set exceedingly high but not unreal expectations. And by quitting school I was throwing away every gift I had inherited.

Trouble came from another quarter as well. As the eldest—indeed, only—son of a Brahmin family, I had certain responsibilities. There were rituals that it would be my duty to perform on my parents' death, and who knows what dire metaphysical consequences would follow if I neglected them. Could a Buddhist monk do what was needed in this realm? Beyond the ritual responsibilities, there was an even greater obligation at stake, one so fundamental to a son's role that it worried even the least devout family members. Even the atheists had a stake in this one. "If you become a Buddhist monk, can you still marry and have children?"

"I don't know. Probably not." It wasn't something I had ever thought about, but I could feel which way the current was pulling and I was swimming in the opposite direction.

Chacha-ji jumped in. "Why? Even Buddha was married. He had a son."

Once again my answer came from nowhere, instantly, "Yeah, but Buddha left his wife. Who will take care of my wife?" Before I could wonder what I was talking about, Chacha-ji answered without hesitation.

"I will."

I looked at my father across the room, his face frozen in an expression of unutterable sadness. And then the nightmare receded and I felt a strange sense of calm come over me. I was talking, but the words were unfamiliar. I was telling them that our relationship as family was temporary, however close we felt. The conditions that had brought us together would dissolve, and others would arise in their place. There was nothing about this particular constellation of relationships, whether father-son or husband-wife, that would endure forever. We would all die, and nothing we did to help one another could prevent that. Rather than put my faith in such illusory relationships, I had decided to devote myself to agama: spiritual studies, not academics. I was aiming for bodhi—enlightenment—and that was the only work that mattered to me. Everything else was illusion.

It was my grandmother who came to my rescue. Mama, as we called her, had been sitting in the corner, watching, saying nothing. She stood up abruptly, brushed her hands on her sari as if concluding some small task, and announced to the room, "It's over now! Finished! You can all go home!"

She came to me and said quietly, "Let's go eat." I followed her out to the kitchen. Chacha-ji's wife fixed us each a plate and sat down with us, watching me closely.

"You know, something happened out there. That wasn't the Khilari I know so well. You were moving your hands as if . . ." She groped for the words. "You were consoling us." My grandmother said nothing, just nodded.

My father stuck his head in the doorway. "Are you talking sense into him?"

Mama's eyes flashed with disdain. "What do you mean? Weren't you listening to him? He's the one talking sense."

At least I had one ally. My grandmother's protection was a lifeline at a time when I had never felt more vulnerable. She could be fierce, I knew well, but not in the same manner as my mother and aunts and great-aunts, who each in their way girded themselves with authoritarian armor to meet the challenges of being modern women in India. No, Mama's power seemed elemental, anciently rooted, and wildly independent.

When she sat with the other old women, tattooed and smoking their hookah or bidis, the real affairs of the village were settled. Her pronouncements could be scathing, delivered with the confidence of an oracle, then sealed in calm when she visited with Bhu Devi's earthen lump in the temple by the well each morning. She was never too dignified to entice me into dancing silly dances or to make me laugh by pulling faces, all wrinkles and no teeth. She gave the sweetest toothless kisses.

We stayed the night in Muzaffarpur, and the next morning I got up before dawn, as I had done every day at the temple. I went to the kitchen and got chai and two biscuits to bring to Mama. That was our ritual during summers in the village. She would feed the cows in the yard before she ate a bite herself, and the birds too had to be fed first. She would break the first biscuit into crumbs and call to the crows in their own language to come eat. There were no cows to feed at my uncle's house. It was more city than village here, and the birds in that snake-infested garden hadn't learned Mama's drill, but she put the crumbs out anyway. "Always remember to offer," she reminded me.

CHAPTER 5

The Testing of Gold

.
.
.

Slowly slowly O mind;
Everything in own pace happens,
Gardener may water a hundred buckets;
Fruit arrives only in its season.

—KABIR

I went back to Kolkata with my parents, feeling like a prisoner dragging his chains. My sisters welcomed me home with tears and scolding, tiptoeing dramatically through the minefields that stretched between my parents and myself. The three of us had always been very close and played together easily despite our age differences; we had learned to rely on one anothers' company when our frequent moves left friends behind. The worst-case scenarios of my disappearance horrified them, as did the pain I had inflicted on my parents. Shefali was a teenager then, mature enough to understand the real risks of my adventure, and to inhabit both sides of the argument. You could see the lawyer she would become. She defended me to my parents, argued for my right to choose my own path, then turned around and advocated on their behalf to me. "A spiritual life is noble, yes, but you're just a kid. You don't know how the world works. You're too young to think about such things, and certainly too young to be traipsing across the country all alone!"

In my own mind, I was no longer a child, having already made the most serious decision any individual could possibly make. I had given up this mundane world! Why couldn't they understand? My younger sister Shilpa was truly the little kid. She was just six then, and she idolized me. She clung to me as if I might disappear again at any moment, and she knew too that her hero had done something bad, which of course was fascinating in its ambiguity.

Returning to boarding school in Asansol was not possible—it was obvious I would bolt at the first opportunity. My parents insisted I start school in Kolkata.

"I don't want to go to school. I want to go back to Rajgir."

"That is out of the question at this stage." It was an article of faith for my father that my obsession was a phase that would eventually pass.

Neither of us would budge. My father would hold his tongue diplomatically, but it was only so long before he couldn't resist raising the threat of school again. We might escalate to harsh words and slamming doors or go directly to heavy silence. Either way we would stop talking to each other for a few days, until a thaw produced another opening. He would try again and the cycle would repeat. Doors slammed. Meals were tense, often skipped.

What began as a stubborn rebellion devolved into a prolonged chill of disillusionment. I still saw friends but I begged off of any family activities and spent hours alone in my room, waiting for a solution to our impasse to somehow present itself. My parents realized that they were groping in the dark. Someone suggested that perhaps a psychiatrist could throw some light on the workings of my mind. A psychiatrist was a rare species in those days among the multitude of healers of the spirit that inhabited Kolkata, but the seers and tantrics circling the house had not yet produced a cure, so I was delivered for a couple of visits. I found the experience mildly amusing, which didn't add to the limited confidence my parents had in the process. We didn't continue.

I remembered that Nabatame had mentioned a Japanese temple in Kolkata. I had been too distressed to ask for details at the time. I pored over the phone book in search of a familiar name. It was a mysteriously slim volume to account for a metropolis of more than ten million, and it yielded nothing.

Meanwhile, gossip was traveling like a bad smell on the wind. My father smoldered after encounters that began with the warmest of greetings and then revealed a smirking curiosity masked as friendly concern. "How is your son doing? I hear he found religion. So he will not be following your footsteps into power?"

●

When the tension at home became overwhelming, my only remedy was to walk. Our home was in a modest apartment complex built for the civil service, but in a fine location facing a park with playing fields. On the far side, across a busy road, was the entrance to the green space that surrounds Dhakuria Lake. There was calm in the open waters, a sense of the city held at bay, the buildings banished to a distant rim behind the trees.

And then, one fading dusk as I walked, I thought I heard a sound: a low boom, a steady beat, barely audible. Not my heart, though almost as familiar. I followed the sound, past the lotus pond, past the swimming club, losing it now and then behind the insistent birdsong and the shouts of kids playing. Out of the park and a block farther down Lake Road. The building that boomed with the sound of the drum could have passed for a modest Indian temple, much smaller than the temple at Rajgir. Its whitewash was due for a freshening. I wasn't at all sure if what I'd discovered was what I hoped. The drumming stopped just as I got there. A caretaker was locking the main door and shooed me back out the gate to the street. "Closed!"

I headed back there first thing the next morning. As I rounded a bend by the lake, a cluster of bright yellow and white robes caught my eye in the distance. I ran for them as if my life depended on it, and pulled up panting through my tears in front of Nabatame. Calmly, as if this were the most ordinary encounter, he said, "Come to the temple. We can talk there."

So I had indeed found Fujii Guruji's temple in Kolkata, a mere fifteen minutes' walk from my home. Once inside, there was no question. The building was aging; it had been built in 1935 and was donated by Raja Birla who was also one of Gandhi's biggest funders. But it contained that same aura of intense care and respect I had felt in Rajgir, the same blend of abundance and precise symmetry, the flowers, the dangling gold ornaments, that same face that had appeared so mysteriously in my mind on the altar, and here, seated in front of it all, a statue of the Buddha made of glowing white jade, looking down with the kindest expression.

Nabatame listened to my lament and advised very simply that my parents were right: I really should be going to school, but of course I could come to the temple whenever I had free time. And so began a life precariously balanced between two worlds. I conveyed my surrender to my parents, who found a school that was willing to admit me halfway through the term. It was not the best but good enough. I made my way to the temple whenever I could, leaving home at four in the morning in time for meditation before the dawn prayer session. Many days I came back again after school, did my homework there and stayed for the evening prayer session, walking home after nightfall. My parents kept their disapproval in silence until the next time some provocation rekindled the conflict.

"This nonsense has gone on long enough. You are wasting your life."

"I never wanted to come back from Rajgir. You forced me to be here, so I'm doing what I need to do."

"You are aiming for a life of poverty and you have no idea what that means. I'm paying for the roof over your head, your food, your clothing."

I pulled off my shirt and threw it at my father. "You can keep it."

As I headed for the door, a final shot found its target: "If you keep this up I will have those foreign monks deported." The words sank in as my feet pounded the road to the temple. Could my father do that? Yes, he could. It was well within his powers, and not beyond where his anger might reach. I would feel the constant chill of that threat for a very long time.

•

Soon after I had found him, Nabatame vanished again. Communication at the temple was minimal at the best of times and it took me a while before I could piece together that he had left to work on a project in Nepal. The elderly monk who was in charge of the Kolkata temple never spoke a word to me.

Every effort I made to connect with Reverend Shinozaki was met with daunting silence. If I tried chatting away regardless, and mentioned Nabatame or Rajgir he would lean forward a little, recognition flickering. When he chanted and beat the large drum, I would sit down uninvited beside him and join in with the small hand drum that Nabatame had given me. The rest of the time he buried his face in a book or the Japanese newspaper, which was at least a week old by the time it reached him. And yet his presence had a cordial warmth. He didn't ignore me, he was just silent. I could only guess that he spoke no Hindi or English, though I learned that he had lived in India for thirty, perhaps forty years.

When the Bangladeshi kids showed up, then he beamed. There was an encampment of refugees along the railroad tracks that ran behind the temple, and a ragamuffin gang of dirty little kids routinely swarmed the temple as their playground. Other visitors would raise an eyebrow at the racket, or sidle away from the unwashed throng with a look of disdain, but Shinozaki never scolded them or treated them with anything other than gentle respect. Sometimes they would sit for the prayer session and he would invite one to take a turn on the hand drum. They had learned to show up about ten minutes before the end of the prayers in anticipation of the handful of sweets that Shinozaki would pass out as *prasad*.

Eventually one day he passed the sweets to me and gestured that I should distribute them. That was a victory. Shinozaki's persistent silence was becoming my personal challenge. A few days later I spotted an opportunity. I knew he didn't want anyone besides him to touch the altar, but that meant he had to interrupt his drumming and get up to light a new stick of incense whenever it burned out. He was aging, and getting up and down wasn't that easy. The next time the incense burned to the end, I jumped up quickly and made eye contact with him, as if to say: *Don't stop! I'll take care of this!* I lit the incense. Mission accomplished. Contact was made, even if no words were exchanged. The altar suffered no harm.

My next advance was bolder. At the beginning of one dawn prayer session, I asked Shinozaki if I could beat the big drum. He nodded and moved to a seat on the floor. I took his place. I brought the stick down on the drumhead with the most satisfying sense of release, the vibration rumbling through my body. The old walls above us shook with delight. Shinozaki offered a glimmer of a smile in approval. It was an excellent prayer session, I thought to myself, and confirmation came in the form of a gesture that beckoned me to breakfast. A simple meal was provided after the prayer session for those who were staying at the temple. There was often a visitor or two from Japan, perhaps a monk passing through as Nabatame had done. That day we ate in eerie quiet, not a word spoken, with the cook and the watchman staring at me from across the table with unashamed curiosity.

•

Since there was no instruction forthcoming from Shinozaki, I made his every move my lesson. I watched how he cleaned the temple, how he carefully arranged the flowers and tended to the shrine. When he recited the Lotus Sutra, I listened intently, trying to catch familiar phrases in the flow of Japanese and memorize every inflection.

This continued over many more weeks. I showed up. I sat in quietude for long stretches. I joined in the chanting. Once in a while Shinozaki signaled that I could beat the big drum; other times I used the hand drum. I lit the incense, and I handed out sweets as *prasad* to the kids. I sat for the quick, silent breakfast. I watched and I waited for something more to happen, though it never did. I was not tempted to quit, not for a moment, but I was conscious that I was running on the fumes of a promise, a faith that the gears would somehow engage and I would find myself in a different kind of reality. Surely Shinozaki would break his silence and start to teach me what a monk needed to learn. Surely I would find a way to prove that I belonged, that I had a purpose there.

The temple had a small library but, with the exception of a few translations of Fujii Guruji's writings into English, it was entirely in Japanese. It was not until a couple of years later that I was able to start Japanese language classes, and much longer before those books would offer up their secrets. At that time, the World Wide Web was still just a proposal on someone's desk at CERN and finding information required actual legwork. The bookstores in Kolkata turned up nothing. The Sri Lankan Maha Bodhi Society had a substantial library, but it was far from home and they were reluctant to lend books out to a kid or even to let me read there. I found a small Buddhist temple that served the Chinese community that had settled around the leather tanneries in Tangra, but no one there was willing to answer my questions. The Bengal Buddhist Association looked promising at first—who knew there were actually Indian Buddhists?—but they too were impenetrable.

Though I was trying hard to learn more about Buddhism, I hadn't closed my mind to other possibilities, regardless of what my parents assumed, and information regarding my own roots was far more easily available. I was inspired by Swami Vivekananda, who was the only Hindu teacher I was aware of who broke the familiar Brahmanical mold by being young, well educated, and attuned to the wider world. I made a weekly trek to the temple he had founded at Belur on the far side of Kolkata to attend private tutorials that Swami Ranga-nathananda was teaching on Advaita Vedanta and Kashmiri Shaivism. I was a seeker. If my understanding of the philosophy was basic at that age, the devotional tone of what I was learning resonated deeply in my being. It also found expression in the songs that I first heard from Baul singers wandering on the train and then tracked down to their community in Kolkata. I pressed them to teach me and I sang like they did about the crazy devotee on the riverbank calling the name of the Lord over and over in ecstasy, or the funny song that pictured Allah, Hari, Ram, and Kali sharing a table together in a restaurant. When I teased them that their anklets were what women wore, they corrected me: "There is no such thing as women or men. The divine is alive inside every body."

Lessons appeared spontaneously too. There was a sadhu who showed up every few days in the park, trailed by a strangely orderly queue of a few dozen stray dogs. He wore a white dhoti and T-shirt, and his gray hair was matted into dreadlocks that were tucked inside the neck of his shirt and tailed out at the bottom. He carried a big box of the cheapest biscuits in his cloth bag. He would sit and the dogs would sit, quietly, patiently, as he called each of them, one by one. He inquired of each one very gently, very politely, about its health, its family, how its day was going, just as if he were speaking to a person. To some he offered a few words of guidance, expressed with love, and he fed each one a biscuit as if he were a priest giving communion. When that task was complete, he would take out a spoon and a small bag of sugar, and sprinkle it on the anthills by the path. I looked out for him, tried to anticipate his coming, and bought biscuits to add to his. His manner and the dogs' respectful patience were mesmerizing to me.

I went looking for Mother Teresa, who had sparked my curiosity when she visited our school in Asansol. I knew a couple of boys there who had originally come from her orphanage. I found Nirmal Hriday, her "house of pure heart," which was a couple of kilometers' walk from home and I spent time on the weekends watching the goings-on quietly from a corner. Occasionally I would have the opportunity to help out with a simple task like moving beds, but there was usually a surplus of volunteers, many of them foreigners. Once I took the opportunity to ask Mother Teresa about the pin she was wearing. She told me it was Saint Francis and explained that he was a saint who had inspired her, and who cared for animals, like dogs and wolves, as well as people. Her words brought to mind the sadhu feeding the dogs, and though I've learned much more about Saint Francis since then, his image has bonded in my mind with the sadhu in the park in Kolkata.

Mostly I was just a fly on the wall, trying to understand what it was that moved through this woman and rippled out over the family of strangers she had gathered around herself; trying to understand how it was that a religious life expressed itself in this intimate commitment—all this feeding, washing, touching, caring—to human beings who were at the most extreme bottom rung of poverty and precarity. It was a kindness, without boundaries or bias, that didn't flinch at sights that most of the world turned their eyes from. And yet she was fiercely bossy and stubborn. Was that a side effect of celebrity, I wondered, or was it necessary to getting the job done?

Not that the job would ever be done, not that way. I was no stranger to the debate about how to cure India's poverty. My family argued fluently in the language of policy, with the conviction that education would shift the story. They did not lack for passion to turn their ideas into action or their resources to charity. What I witnessed at the "house of pure heart" was very different. Solving systemic problems was not the agenda. The nuns' vow of poverty would not serve to end anyone else's poverty, and their medical care was rudimentary at best. But that didn't matter. What they offered was not scalable, practical solutions so much as a potion concocted of love, dignity, human warmth, and attention. On its own terms, on its own scale, it worked miracles.

•

Six long months after I first came to the temple, Shinozaki finally broke his silence. We had finished the morning prayers and were sitting down to breakfast, just the two of us that day, when he turned to me and said in halting Hindi, but with an expression of uncomplicated pleasure, *"Yah ek sundar din hai, hai na?"* "It's a beautiful day, isn't it?" It was indeed. A most beautiful April morning with the flame trees bursting into blossom in the park and my heart flooded with gratitude and relief in that moment.

It wasn't as if Shinozaki suddenly became loquacious after that. We never did have the deep philosophical discussions that I longed for. But there was a genuine thaw. He seemed happy to see me each morning, and offered tokens of trust wrapped up in small requests: Could you change the flowers in the shrine today? Would you polish the statue a bit? Now and again he offered a few words of encouragement. Sometimes we even went for long walks together in the park without a word needing to pass between us.

Little by little I was spending more time at the temple. My parents grudgingly granted permission for me to sleep there a couple of nights a week, avoiding some of the walking to and from home in the dark and the monsoon rains. I kept up my side of the bargain. I transferred to a better school, got good grades, won debates, excelled at sports. On the surface I was doing well, but the effort of constantly shuttling between two worlds was exhausting.

Our truce was fragile, and my parents periodically mounted fresh attacks in unexpected ways. My mother's strategy was spiritual diversion. The family went on a long road trip to Ajmer to visit the shrine of the Sufi saint Moinuddin Chishti. I remember the press of the crowd, the noise, the fluorescent tube lights eerie with their wrapping of green cellophane, the smell of frankincense, and then somehow slipping into a sense of profound peace in the midst of the chaos. I think Ma's intention was to suggest that religion was a broad and diverse realm and one ought not to focus with too narrow a fixation on one tradition. Be open-minded and eclectic. Instead of a life commitment, let it be a hobby. Like collecting stamps.

When that failed, she fought fire with fire, her faith against mine. There was a celebrated Aghori, a fiercely ascetic devotee of Shiva, who was much respected by my grandparents. He came to Vishnupur Titirah every ten years and those visits were a special occasion when the entire village would gather to hear him teach. Ma and my auntie dragged me out of the house and sat me down on the veranda in the presence of the great man, with the crowd of about a thousand people seated on the ground before him and the cows tied up at the well completing the picture. My grandmother told him the whole story: the running away, the Japanese monks, drumming and chanting and scrubbing the floor . . . and asked if he could help. The crowd was hushed in anticipation, half expecting to witness a miracle. He looked at me. We locked eyes for what felt like several long minutes without him saying a word. And then those bulging eyes in that fearsome ash-smeared face, framed by his long beard and big earrings, broke into a smile. *"Ye mere vash ke bahar hai . . . shiv iske sath hai."* "He's beyond me. He's with Shiva." We both laughed and the crowd exhaled. Ma looked perplexed. That was the last of her spiritual interventions.

My father's strategy consisted in recruiting respected champions of reason to lean on me. He had plenty of allies who could argue for the true enlightenment of education against the superstitious darkness of religion, but Mamu-nana was his ace in the hole. Known to the world as R. S. Sharma, my mother's uncle was one of India's most eminent historians. He was a professor at the University of Toronto as well as at the universities in Delhi and Patna, senior fellow at London's School of Oriental and African Studies, with a list of other positions and honors as long as both arms and legs. He had pioneered modern methods of data analysis and the use of archaeology to illuminate ancient texts, dismantled much of the colonial mindset that distorted the study of Indian history, brought the role of peasants and women to the foreground, and—at considerable risk to his own life—debunked the mythical pseudo-history that served as propaganda for ethnic strife. He was a giant in his field and a colossus in our family, where many, including my father, had studied under him.

We would often stop at Mamu-nana's home in Patna on the way to our village for the summer holidays, so I didn't suspect an ulterior motive when my parents planned a visit. We sat, as guests always did, in the cane chairs in the small foyer that faced the pomegranate tree, as if the overflow of books that filled every room had edged its inhabitants right out the door. As always, Mamu-nana was dressed in a white dhoti-kurta. If he wore anything else in London and Toronto, which I doubt, we never saw it in India. The very fact that he still made his home in a provincial backwater like Patna was an anomaly for someone of his accomplishment, but his attachment to a simpler life in India's heartland seemed fitting for someone so deeply engaged with its past.

I'd spent many a summer morning—and there were many more to come—sitting in a corner on the floor of that small porch, listening in on Mamu-nana's conversation with visiting colleagues as they debated theory, shared news of a new dig, or untangled the meaning of a particular phrase in an ancient text. But this time I was in the hot seat, not just a listener but a full-fledged discussant. After the requisite inquiries about health and family and such, which were brief because Mamu-nana was never one for small talk, we arrived at the topic of the day. To my surprise, it was Buddhism and how I might best apply myself to learning more about it.

My parents were a little smug at their advantage in having the great man in their camp, and it's true that he argued in favor of education and against my becoming a monk, but his approach was uniquely his own. I don't know if he sensed how hungry for knowledge the silence at the temple had left me, or if he saw a mirror of his own wide-open curiosity in my eagerness, but he laid out a generous feast.

He began with encouragement: There was much that was good about Buddhism, for sure. Mamu-nana's view of history was always filtered through a Marxist lens that focused on economics and modes of production, but his Marxism was born out of a deep concern for social justice. He described the Buddha as leading an egalitarian movement in rebellion against the dominant Hindu beliefs of the time, and delighted in the account of how cleverly he subverted the caste system by controlling the sequence of his disciples' ordination: A prince who became a monk would have to defer to the seniority of a low-caste person who was ordained before him.

The conversation that we began then would continue on and off over many years, and into a time when I brought a more mature understanding to the table, so it's hard to untangle exactly what was said that day from other days, or to gauge how he simplified things to guide a child who had thrown himself headfirst into deep waters and whose parents were desperate for help. But I remember clearly the awe I felt to perceive a window opening on the historical landscape that the Buddha inhabited, and my excitement at learning that I was connected, personally and intimately, to a world I had discerned only dimly through a Japanese filter.

I had understood that Rajgir was a place of importance in the Buddha's life, but I had not realized how deeply that life was rooted in this corner of India, how the roads he walked again and again crisscrossed the familiar landscape of Bihar. Did I know, Mamu-nana asked, that Vaishali, where our village of Vishnupur Titirah was located, was one of the places where the Buddha often taught? Vaishali was where the powerful courtesan Amrapali had gifted a mango grove to the great teacher. I was stunned. Were the mango groves that I played in descended from the same trees that had shaded the Buddha? Had he eaten that same fruit dripping with sweet juice? Did I know—Mamu-nana interrupted my fantasy— that the Magahi dialect my father's family spoke was virtually the same tongue that the Buddha spoke? If I had heard him teach, I could have understood his words easily.

Vaishali was also where one of the Emperor Ashoka's pillars was found, after serving for centuries as a mud-covered hitching post for cattle. Did I know that my name,

Priyadarshi—"he who looks on others with love"—was Ashoka's name too? And that name, deciphered on an ancient stone inscription and matched in an obscure text, was the essential clue that cracked the mystery of the long-vanished story of Buddhism in India. We would study the Mauryan dynasty and Ashoka's pillars in history class the next year, but the textbook version paled beside Mamu-nana's magic.

Beyond the childlike awe, which I've never entirely outgrown, at how ancient stories are still alive in my bones, Mamu-nana planted another seed in my mind that quietly put down roots and would become meaningful later in my life: When Ashoka the conqueror stood on the battlefield at Kalinga—the corpses mixed with those still groaning, the sky dark with vultures—and felt his heart moved to profound regret, he didn't renounce the empire he had won and go off into the forest to be a monk, though he probably considered that option. Precedent and culture would have made it a reasonable choice. Instead, he stayed on the job. He worked at bringing his understanding of the Buddha's teachings into the realm of governance, and what he accomplished is remembered as a golden age in India's past. Here was evidence that Buddhist ethics could be put into practice as the foundation for a just and healthy society. In choosing to commit myself to a spiritual path, I had assumed that turning away from the world was a requirement. But here was a glimpse, down the tunnel of centuries, of a choice that was different but no less worthy.

Of course, there was a downside too, and Mamu-nana didn't spare me the negatives. To a Marxist, the monks' disengagement from economic production was damnably confounding. Their rituals were so much hocus-pocus and superstition. And the corruption that riddled the once-great monasteries, which came to harbor thieves disguised in robes, was as much to blame for the complete erasure of Buddhism from its homeland as any invading army. But the real reason he warned me against becoming a monk had to do with his own deeply felt sense of what constitutes intellectual excellence. The price of entry to this tantalizing store of knowledge that we were peeking into was an open mind, and I would forfeit the spirit of independent inquiry if I were to become a monk. If I really wanted to learn about Buddhism, he insisted, I should approach it as a scholar, not as a monk. The bias of a believer would inevitably compromise my objectivity and the results would be second-rate.

I didn't have the language yet to answer him. I had little to refer to beyond the booming of the drum, syllables recited in a foreign tongue, and what I could glean from the behavior of Nabatame and Shinozaki. I couldn't pull from a pile of books to clarify a thought, confirm a reference, quote a text, as Mamu-nana did so easily. But I knew instinctively that the two realms of faith and intellect didn't have to be mutually exclusive. Somehow it should be possible to become a monk without making a sacrificial offering of one's brain. If Mamunana could be an internationally acclaimed scholar who jetted from one university to another and yet remained grounded in a sleepy town in Bihar, then maybe I could be a monk who could think for myself. The world didn't simply collapse in the face of strange contradictions.

What I didn't yet know was that a reliance on empirical evidence and logical analysis, rather than blind faith, was woven into the fabric of Buddhist thought from its beginnings. The Buddha advised his followers not to take his teachings on faith: *Burn them, smash them, test their purity as a goldsmith would test the purity of gold.* In other words, subject them to the furnace of reason and observe them in the laboratory of experience. Find out for yourself what their effects are. Do they help to reduce your suffering? Do they make you more skillful in reducing others' suffering? Do they make you more free?

Invoking a goldsmith's tests suggests a reaching for scientific objectivity that controverts stereotypes of religious dogma, and that passage has been a favorite of those who are invested in the idea that Buddhism, among the world's religions, is somehow specially suited to rational modernity. But the invitation to test the gold is not exactly a claim to objectivity. In fact, the Buddha's teaching constantly calls into question our assumptions about the very nature of objectivity.

Every one of the sutras—the accounts of the Buddha's teaching that have come down to us—begins with the phrase *Evam maya shrutam* . . . "Thus have I heard . . ." That opening, hedged as one listener's experience, implies that this is just one possible account of what happened, filtered by a human mind and the limitations of memory. As scripture goes, it's a rather tentative beginning. What typically follows next is a sketch of the setting: where the Buddha was staying at the time, who was present to hear him speak, what occasion or questions led to his words. This record offers a glimpse of the Buddha's daily life: Amidst the communal routine of meditation, the alms round, the daily meal, there was time when monks or visitors could bring their questions to the teacher. His sermons were not composed in advance, but arose organically in response to those questions. The Buddha's words were often attuned to the needs of a particular audience, a particular time and place. Although some of the Buddha's teachings are considered *nitartha,* or clearly definitive, a great many are described as *neyartha,* conditional and open to interpretation. They are not divine revelation, absolute and incontrovertible, but communication skillfully framed for a particular audience. It was emphasized again and again that each listener heard those words differently, according to their own capacity and their own concerns.

Our encounter with those words today is not meant to be a passive experience any more than it was when they were first uttered. The invitation stands: Test the teachings. We are free to argue and grapple with them intellectually. Doubt is not heresy; it is a necessary part of the process. It is no accident that debate was at the core of how learning was structured traditionally in Buddhist monasteries, or that the formal logic of philosophical debate was finely honed there. And so, with hindsight, I could have said to Mamu-nana that he didn't need to worry: I had not signed up for a cultish lobotomy.

More to the point, intellectual understanding will never provide the complete picture. If we are genuinely going to bite into the gold, we need to test it in ways that are not just theoretical but grounded in experience. That internalized, living knowledge requires practice. As delighted as I was by what I could glean from Mamu-nana's attempt to entice me into the scholars' camp, and in spite of my hunt for books in all corners of Kolkata, I knew that book knowledge was not sufficient to the goal of spiritual learning. There was a reason I had headed for the train station first and the library later. You can learn all there is to know about the physics and biomechanics that go into riding a bicycle, and fill the blackboard with formulas and equations, but until you get in the seat and make the effort, until you fall off a few times and get back on, whatever you can say about riding a bike will fall short of even a child's experience. Besides, even if one's goal were a purely scholarly understanding of Buddhism in its historical context—knowledge on Mamu-nana's terms—surely having personal insight into the spiritual experience at the heart of the historical phenomenon would be an advantage, not a handicap.

There is a place and a purpose for faith, but it doesn't stand in opposition to inquiry and it's far more effective when it's not blind. The spiritual path is a trek into the unknown, and the unknown is a scary place. It's also a path of indeterminate length. It might take many years, or perhaps many lifetimes, and the destination may not be quite where we thought we were headed at the beginning. Faith is a cloak of confidence that keeps us moving forward, one foot in front of the other, even when the journey seems uncertain or veers off into the unmapped, dragon-infested territory of our actual lives and relationships. Faith is what launched me out the doors of St. Vincent's, what kept me scrubbing floors at Rajgir, and what drew me back to the temple, day after day, when Shinozaki seemed unapproachable and disinterested.

A good part of faith is patience and perseverance, and those qualities, curiously, are qualities essential to practice. The musician repeating scales over and over might seem to be carrying out a stupefying ritual until you understand how that practice relates to musical performance. Just as faith supports practice, practice also feeds faith. When we begin to see the effects, however small, of practice over time—when we find that practice has made us just a tiny bit calmer, more compassionate, more focused, less judgmental—that positive feedback tells us: Eureka! This is gold.

CHAPTER 6

The Torchbearers

.
.
.

> I do not accept any absolute formulas for living.
> No preconceived code can see ahead to
> everything that can happen in a man's life. As we
> live, we grow and our beliefs change. They must
> change. So I think we should live with this
> constant discovery. We should be open to this
> adventure in heightened awareness of living. We
> should stake our whole existence on our
> willingness to explore and experience.
>
> —MARTIN BUBER

I found my way back to Rajgir during the first school vacation, this time with my parents' permission. It was not as simple as that sounds. I planned, lobbied, and argued my cause for weeks in advance, with all the diplomacy I could muster. I was persistent but careful to avoid fireworks. I didn't want to provoke my father's anger or renew his threat to deport the monks.

In the end, they conceded. It was a pattern that would repeat for almost every school break of sufficient length to travel. Rajgir was my Christmas, my Dussehra and Diwali, and every return was a homecoming. Each time I arrived, the tension that I had been carrying for months—the defensive stance that became second nature against my parents' relentless press, and the sadness at always being wrong in their eyes—all fell away and dissolved in the breeze as I hiked the last mile of the stone staircase up the hill.

That first trip back I wasn't sure who I would find there; as far as I knew Nabatame was still in Nepal. From the bus station I made a beeline "upstairs." I wanted most of all to pay my respects at the peak. I was intercepted, however, by one of the laborers who brought me "downstairs" with instructions to report to *mataji*—"mother"—as he called her.

"Mother" was an elderly Japanese nun who was so tiny, so polite, and so dignified that it's hard to explain how intimidating she could be when the occasion demanded. She wanted to know who I was. I tried to explain myself. The laborer was put on the spot to translate, but his Japanese was no better than mine. Finally, we had a breakthrough. She was pointing at my hand drum, repeating her question. And I understood. "Nabatame-shounin," I answered. She responded with a beaming smile and signaled for me to sit and wait. The next thing I knew we were having lunch. It was unusually convivial for a temple meal, with actual conversation mediated by her son, Reverend Okonogi, who spoke Hindi as fluently as any native. I learned that he was in fact the abbot of the temple, that his mother had lived there since it was first built, and they had only been away on a trip when I first came, with Nabatame looking after things for them.

From that point on, I was one of the family. Anju-sama, or "reverend nun" as I learned to call her, would become as close to me as a grandmother. My parents eventually came to understand and accept how central she was in my life. I doubt they realized how often she urged me to be kinder to them. Okonogi became a big brother, a lifelong friend whose lessons were so woven into the fabric of daily life and so humbly presented that they were almost imperceptible.

Our routine was simple. Every day began in darkness. Anju-sama slept near the shrine room and was always the first up, fresh and ready by three-thirty in the morning. The beat of the drum, the chanting and the recitation of the sutra welcomed the dawn, and we circled the stupa as the rising sun washed it in a glow of pink and gold. At the edge of the terrace we would bow to Vulture Peak where the platform atop the hill was visible below us. Then on to Fujii Guruji's room, where prayers would conclude, followed by breakfast. Right after breakfast we would go into cleaning mode, then more recitation, chanting, beating the drum. After another break, there was more of the same, and again into the evening.

All of our meals were very brief and spartan, but prepared and served with the utmost care. Anju-sama could make a dish of plain rice and a single vegetable taste like the most elegant offering. Every breakfast of chai and chapatis was a heartwarming feast.

Sometimes I would hike with Anju-sama to the terrace at Vulture Peak. She was as tiny and delicate as a little bird, and the wind sweeping up from the plains below threatened to lift her away in a sudden gust. I held on to her to keep her safe. I was big for my age. Even as a child, I was more substantial than she was. There, on the clearing at the rocky promontory surrounded by a vast view, that same feeling of vibrant calm that had mesmerized me on my first visit returned every time. When the wind dropped, as if suspended for a moment in the sky, my breath would almost stop, I so wanted not to shatter the perfect clarity of the sheer light. I pictured the Buddha speaking to the circle of monks who sat listening intently. I could almost hear words and phrases, the language familiar, a voice resonating inside my bones.

Not only Vulture Peak but all of Rajgir seemed to contain memories of the past glowing just beneath the surface of the present. I learned that the caves I had discovered below the peak when I first arrived were indeed where the monks went to meditate, and there were many other caves in the hills around us that had also sheltered the monks as they practiced. The cave I had chosen for myself was special to Ananda, the Buddha's cousin and attendant whose remarkable memory helped to preserve so many of the teachings. It is his voice, so often, that echoes in the opening words of the sutras, *Thus have I heard . . .*

The downstairs temple was surrounded by what once had been the bamboo grove, Venuvana, where the monks' huts became the first beginnings of something like a monastery. It was the haven where they gathered for the monsoon. Whenever it rained, but especially in that same season when heavy curtains of water swept across the plain, I imagined how they all settled in for three months of quiet and meditation under the dripping leaves of the bamboo grove, going nowhere till the monsoon ended for another year.

❧

Tak! The sound of the wooden block that punctuated the recitation woke me. I sat bolt upright, thinking I had overslept. *Tak!* But no, it was still the middle of the night, the moon high. Who was reciting at this hour? I could recognize phrases, it was the same sixteenth chapter of the sutra that we had been reciting earlier . . . *Isshin yoku ken butsu* . . . "with one heart, single-minded, longing to see the Buddha . . ."

At breakfast, I asked Okonogi if there had been some special ceremony. Why the chanting so late at night? He laughed, then exchanged a few words in Japanese with his mother. They both looked at me. Anju-sama was beaming. "Very few people have heard that," Okonogi said. They had both been sound asleep.

"So I imagined it?"

"No, you probably heard someone."

"You mean there really was someone reciting in the temple last night?"

"There are all kinds of things that happen, and sometimes you just encounter them." Okonogi guessed that it was probably Fujii Guruji. An elderly monk who knew the venerable teacher well had heard the same chanting late at night when he stayed at the temple. I wasn't sure what to make of this. Whatever I had heard, clearly Anju-sama and Okonogi were both quietly pleased.

•

When we did our cleaning in the temple, Anju-sama would talk to the statues as she polished them, and every morning she would sit for a while in front of the scroll painting of Nichiren and share her thoughts with the great Japanese Buddhist teacher who lived eight centuries ago. She chattered softly in tones that were affectionate, intimate, as if she were talking to a dear friend, but also deeply respectful. The statues and paintings were not inert objects for her, nor even mere symbols, but somehow doorways through which one could catch a glimpse of the enlightened beings they represented. Just as a photograph can unlock a store of memories from the way an expression flickers across a familiar face, these images had captured qualities that one could learn from.

The fact that she spoke only Japanese didn't matter. She would talk to me much as she talked to the statues, and I responded as best I could with gestures and facial expressions. The stream of gentle sounds seemed precise and exquisitely polite to my ears. Languages come easily to me. Between the frequent moves the family made for my father's job and our summers in the village, I could mimic the Bengali I'd heard on the streets of Asansol and Kolkata, or the Gujarati of Ahmadabad. I was at home in the Angika, Bhojpuri, and Magahi of my family's base in Bihar, and of course Hindi and English were a given. Japanese was unlike any other language I had attempted, but I had been listening intently for months to the chanting of the sutras. A familiar name or phrase would offer a brief foothold here and there, but for the most part I would wade into Anju-sama's burbling stream, and let the sounds wash over me until somehow the current would carry me and her stories would start to make sense.

*

When Anju-sama and her husband, Okonogi's father, first encountered the Most Venerable Nichidatsu Fujii, they were stunned by the sheer intensity of his presence and the single-minded extremity of his determination, as much as by his humility. It was during the years of poverty and humiliation that followed Japan's defeat in the war, and he was no longer young, though age never slowed him. He was almost seventy then, and he would yet live to be a hundred.

He seemed utterly fearless. He had chosen to become a monk at a time when Buddhism was being suppressed and discredited by the Meiji government. He walked a path of radical pacifism, speaking out against war even as Japan's national pride was pouring itself into military expansion.

Though he had studied deeply with many different schools, he put aside books and sought experience in ascetic practices, fasting strictly and chanting for days under waterfalls. His main practice was simplicity itself: He walked the city streets and country roads, beating his drum, and chanting the prayer that contained the essence of the Lotus Sutra. His method was to reach out and touch hearts, one by one, in unshakeable faith that the foundation of world peace was for each of us to hold all others in deep affection and respect.

Until they met Fujii Guruji, what Anju-sama and her husband had held in deepest affection and respect was each other. And so the couple decided together to dedicate their lives and their still-young marriage to this work. Fujii Guruji ordained them both, and because Anju-sama was already pregnant with a little Okonogi at the time, a third person was ordained that day. Whatever the rules might say, the child in her belly was not separate from her when she took the vows. In any case, her son was born and raised among monks and nuns in the small temple that they made of their home in Chiba, and he never knew any other life outside the order.

Okonogi, all grown up now, stood in the doorway, dumbfounded. "Why do you just sit there nodding? Can you understand what she's saying?"

"Sort of. She's talking about Fujii Guruji and how she and your father were ordained together, and then you were born . . ."

He shook his head in amazement.

The devastation that Fujii Guruji witnessed in the war, and especially the unspeakable suffering of Hiroshima and Nagasaki, so moved him that he made worldwide disarmament his mission. He had never been daunted by impossible tasks; there was simply no way not to act. "The time has come," he said, "when we can no longer contain the urge to do something, but rush out of our houses. The time has come to look up to heaven, prostrate ourselves to earth, to voice our grief, and to share it with everyone." Walking and chanting was not enough. He decided to build stupas to serve as beacons pointing a path to peace; they would be outposts of the Buddha's pure realm superimposed on this sad earth.

The first stupa was built on Mount Hanaoka in Japan in the aftermath of the war, and took eight years of labor, his own and that of a handful of followers and war orphans he recruited. They used hand tools and worked barefoot, on rations barely a notch above starvation. When it was finished, many tens of thousands of people came to the opening for a ceremony that marked a renewal of hope. The second stupa was the marvelous structure that had surprised me here at Rajgir, on the hill called Ratnagiri—Jewel Peak—overlooking Vulture Peak.

Fujii Guruji had first come to India in 1931, determined to fulfill the prophecy that Nichiren had made seven centuries earlier: that Buddhism would return to India from Japan, after having been erased from the land of its origin for centuries. When he met with Gandhi face-to-face, two kindred spirits recognized each other. The lack of a common language was no barrier to easy laughter, tears of joy, and expressive silence. It was Gandhi who first addressed him as Guruji—"respected teacher"—and the title stuck, though Guruji came away from his stay at Gandhi's ashram in Wardha a little humbler than when he first arrived. He learned that India was not as primitive as he had assumed, and had not entirely let go of the thread of the Buddha's teachings of ahimsa. As Gandhi spun his cotton while they sat together, Guruji witnessed a sublime light radiating from the wooden wheel, and he understood how Gandhi was spinning a new fabric of independence from ancient principles of nonviolence.

Gandhi delighted in Guruji's drumming and incorporated the Japanese chant of *namu myoho renge kyo* into the twice-daily interfaith prayer meeting at his ashram. Fujii Guruji's big drum also laid a rhythm at meetings of the Indian National Congress. When the Japanese army had already won Burma and offered to join with the independence movement in ousting the British from India, and Subhas Chandra Bose was recruiting an army with a call for blood as the price of freedom, it was the Japanese monks who pleaded with Gandhi. They felt that Japan, with its militant drive and dictatorial ambitions, had lost its way and was not to be trusted, and the monks helped to sway the decision against inviting the Japanese army into India.

Fujii Guruji visited Rajgir when he first came to India. Animals grazed where the large temple now stands and tigers roamed the hills where he climbed through the brush in the dark each morning to watch the sun rise at Vulture Peak. He made a vow: This spot was where the Buddha's teaching would begin to find its way back to India. After the war, when India had won independence and travel restrictions on the Japanese were eventually lifted, he returned, and Prime Minister Nehru asked him to help with plans to restore Rajgir as a place of pilgrimage. The construction of the stupa at Rajgir was only marginally easier than the first stupa in Japan, though there were many more people helping. Every bit of cement and gravel, and the water to mix them, had to be carried by hand the three miles up to the site. And the chairlift, which Nehru had specifically requested, also had to be built.

After her husband died, Anju-sama followed Fujii Guruji to India. Once she reached Vulture Peak, she wanted never to leave again. She would die here happily, she said. Her son followed when he was seventeen, and Fujii Guruji ordained him again, properly this time. Okonogi spent a few years in Orissa, building yet another stupa, until he was appointed abbot at Rajgir. The closeness between Anju-sama and Okonogi, and the loving care of their relationship, set the mood in Rajgir. Seeing them together made me feel even more rooted there.

Okonogi was often busy with the responsibilities of his administrative role. The temple and stupa see a steady traffic of tourists and pilgrims daily, and over the years I have watched him organize celebrations that demanded months of work in advance, with visiting dignitaries and big crowds straining the very limited local infrastructure. But whatever else is happening, he is always there to lead the prayers, in the darkness and solitude every morning before dawn, regardless of how late he has arrived the night before or how jetlagged he is. Punctuality is a particular fetish of his, or more precisely, an expression of mindfulness and dedication. In all the years I have known him, he has never once shown up for a train less than twenty-five minutes in advance. I've waited with him on the platform countless times, laughing out loud at this ritual.

In spite of his obsession with the clock, he taught me that practice is not something you do at a particular hour, separate from the rest of your life. It is never just recitation and chanting and drumming. Practice is a container and if done right, everything we do, every waking moment, is held inside that container. Every detail of the simplest act, from folding a cloth to picking up a teapot, is worth doing carefully, correctly, with patience and full attention. I think it was part of Oko-nogi's own practice to remain ever so steadfastly patient as he taught me to do things right, including the hours we spent on the teapot. His attentiveness was a gift that meant the world to me. Of all the Japanese monks I came to know, he was the only one who picked up the local language beyond a few words for survival, out of a desire to connect with people. In a culture where silence was the norm, he was willing to talk and comfortable doing so. Without preaching or proselytiz-ing, he made everyone feel welcome.

It was Anju-sama who first gave me a hint of what the words we had been reciting all this time might signify. It wasn't until three years after my first trip to Rajgir that I was able to come by an English translation of the Lotus Sutra. I had begged the monks who traveled back and forth to Japan to bring me a translation, but they had always declined, politely but with-out wavering. "Just practice," they told me. "English will only give you the words, it won't give you the meaning of the sutra." And as if to prove them right, when I finally received the precious, long-awaited text, and opened it—after first wrapping it in a silk cloth and placing it on my shrine at home in anticipation of a perfectly auspicious full moon—it still mystified me.

The setting was at Vulture Peak, but it seemed to be a dif-ferent universe, a cosmic playground of kaleidoscopic multi-plicity, where the circle of monks that I envisioned was joined by thousands—no, hundreds of thousands—no, now it's millions—of celestial beings crowding the sky. Logic circled on itself not unlike the heavenly robes they tossed on high, tumbling over and over, and worlds were measured out in mathematical games of infinitude. There was not just the Buddha who had lived and taught here some two and a half millennia ago, but Buddhas beyond number who had lived through all time. All this was reported in an opaquely foreign English that talked of "timely tactfulness" and much else that stymied me.

Meanwhile, Anju-sama helped. She shared what amounted to the first fragments of commentary that helped me to make sense of what I was hearing in Japanese. She answered my questions, explained a word here, a phrase there. She extracted and retold the passages that were most meaningful to her, and her alchemy turned stories into gold. Her favorite was the Bodhisattva Fukyo, a monk who neither studied nor recited. Instead, he stood at the temple gate bowing in reverence to anyone and everyone who passed by, saying "I bow to you because you will be a Buddha one day." He made no distinction between monks or laymen, men or women, and he bowed with equal reverence to a dog, a cat, a donkey. For his efforts he was mocked and beaten, but he never gave up, and he bowed equally to those who beat him—though from a safe distance—for they too would be Buddhas one day. As would he, the sutra explains.

Even stranger, the alchemy didn't end there: That one day was no other day than now. All those future Buddhas, whether dogs and donkeys or difficult human beings, were going about their business here and now. As the language of the sutra became familiar, it felt less like exploring a text and more like discovering a universe that pervaded the very air around us. Right here a perfect, loving, otherworldly harmony rubbed elbows with the mundane and the miserable. There was no pure land of peace in some other place, some future time, that I needed to find my way to. I held it in my own mind, my own heart.

CHAPTER 7

Snakes and Scorpions

.

.

.

As long as space remains
And living beings endure
May I too remain
To dispel the miseries of this world.

—SHANTIDEVA

The summer before my junior year of high school, I decided
to visit Nabatame in Nepal. I knew that he was in charge of
building a stupa and temple in Lumbini, the Buddha's birth-
place. My parents wouldn't hear of me traveling to Nepal.
Absolutely not! But by then they were resigned to my absences
in Rajgir, so I went to Nepal via a couple days' detour to Rajgir, where I convinced Okonogi to give me the bus fare to
Lumbini.

I walked across the border at Raxaul at around four in the
morning after endless bus rides, and then hired a horse cart to
get to the bus station on the Nepali side. Not having enough
cash to pay bribes made it easy to push back. *Main Hindu-
stani hoon!* I wasn't some rich tourist they could hit up for

baksheesh. Locals didn't even need a passport to cross. Customs? How could a small backpack with a change of clothes and a few books be a problem?

I got to Lumbini and located the temple, which was a construction site with a small colony of huts that housed some of the workers. There was no way I could have phoned ahead, and as it happened Nabatame was away when I arrived. The young Sri Lankan monk who was left in charge wanted nothing to do with this oddly insistent young tourist. I spent the night at a nearby guesthouse that served pilgrims and the day loitering at the construction site, feeling entirely unwelcome.

When Nabatame returned, he was shocked to see me. "Did you run away again?"

"Sort of."

"What does that mean?"

"My parents think I'm in Rajgir." The fact that Okonogi was complicit, if not exactly responsible for my being there, was in my favor. Nabatame said I could stay if I didn't mind sleeping on a mat on the ground, which was fine by me. He assigned me to share a hut with the Sri Lankan monk.

The next morning over breakfast we discussed how I might be useful. "The cook has quit," Nabatame said. "Do you know how to cook?" There were around thirty laborers who had to be fed daily. I confessed that I'd never had a reason to spend time in the kitchen. My mother was an exceptionally good cook, and she had all the help she needed.

"What about carpentry then?"

"I've never hammered a nail."

"Laying bricks?" I shook my head. No experience there either. "It seems you've lived a very sheltered life."

He spoke the words lightly, but they cut. I went back to the hut under a dark cloud. Having come all this way, this was not how things were supposed to play out. That Brahmin kid who wouldn't get his hands dirty was not who I was. My mind was filled with stories of the hardship Fujii Guruji went through to build the first stupas. This was holy work and I was hungry to have a part in it.

I came back out and told Nabatame that even though I brought with me no relevant skills, I was willing to learn. I was young and strong. He nodded and sent me off with a group of laborers. I made myself useful carrying bricks, cement, and sand from one spot to another, and they taught me to mix mortar for the masonry.

∗

Early one morning before the laborers were normally up, we were doing prayers in Nabatame's hut when screams broke through the chanting. A cobra had made its nest in the carpenters' hut and caused a panic when one of the men woke up and saw it. The commotion continued with heated discussion. Everybody had an opinion about the habits of cobras. Everybody had a story to tell about a prior encounter with a snake. Everybody had a theory about the best way to kill it.

At that, Nabatame drew the line. They could move the hut or build another one, lay down all the marigolds and green chilies they pleased, but there would be no killing of cobras or anything else that happened to slither, crawl, or creep inside. This did not go down well. Everyone had seen Nabatame escorting a scorpion, held delicately with a pair of chopsticks, to the edge of the clearing behind the huts where our encampment faced the jungle. This removal and liberation happened on many occasions. Even Nabatame's hut, which contained the altar, offered little protection from anything other than weather. To the Nepali laborers, the expert gesture with the chopsticks seemed an eccentricity of their Japanese boss, who had specific notions about the right way to do many things. Cohabiting with cobras was a step too far, they grumbled.

"The cobras lived here before we came," Nabatame told them. "We are the intruders." My own fear of snakes wrestled with my respect for Nabatame. But it was true: Until archaeologists discovered the pillar that Ashoka had raised here, this holy place was abandoned. Scorpions and cobras were its caretakers. The park where the Buddha's mother Mayadevi steadied herself against a sala tree as she delivered him into the world had long ago dissolved into the forest that surrounded us. The only reason for our undertaking here was to honor the Buddha's teaching. The first and most important precept that he taught was to abstain from killing or harming living beings. If we killed to build the stupa—if the means did not respect the end—the whole project would be a failure.

●

I had come to Nepal to see Nabatame with high hopes of learning something in the way of a monk's education. The construction work offered certain valuable life lessons; tamping concrete can tamp ego too. But I had plenty of questions saved up and I tried to engage Nabatame whenever we had a break. When my questions veered toward the philosophical, he would return to the same refrain I had heard over and over again from the monks in Fujii Guruji's order: "Don't worry about that. Just practice. When you beat the drum, you will begin to understand."

And yet Nabatame could see that I didn't have time to practice after the long hours of tiring physical work. He called me into his hut one day and said, "I think you should go to Pokhara. There is an unbuilt stupa there, but you won't need

to do construction. It's a very quiet place where you can practice. There is nobody there to lead the prayers right now, so
that would be your responsibility."

He put me on the bus alongside a Japanese hippie who was
a delightfully colorful companion for the daylong ride. I was
intrigued that he carried no luggage beyond an array of light-
ers and many cartons of cigarettes that he was chain-smoking
as we climbed slowly through the forested lower reaches of
the Himalayas. When we arrived at Pokhara, the beauty of
the stupa's site took my breath away. It was high on a wooded
hill above Lake Phewa, with the town below lapping the eastern shore of the lake. All across the horizon the snow-dusted
white peaks of the Annapurna range divided earth from sky.

What Nabatame called an "unbuilt" stupa was exactly
that. Construction had begun some twenty years earlier and
then halted. Hindu authorities, who were not happy that Nepal's Buddhist history was being honored, ordered the monks
to leave and demolished the stupa. By the time I was there, the
recent democratic transition had made it possible for construction to resume. The temple and a couple of guest rooms
were complete, and a contractor was slowly rebuilding the
stupa with a small team of laborers who came and went during the day. There was a Gurkha armed with a kukri knife
who served as watchman and another caretaker who I had to
eject the day he showed up horribly drunk. Mostly I was
alone. Though the stupa has become a busy tourist attraction
now, very few visitors ever came up the hill in those days.

I threw myself wholeheartedly into what was, essentially,
my first solo retreat. The practice became effortless. I could
beat the drum for nine hours straight without fatigue. Distractions disappeared. The recitation of the sutra was intoxi-

cating. We talk about how focus narrows, but the reality is that when all else is excluded what you are focusing on expands, its every detail larger, richer, more fully present. There was nothing but the frictionless funnel of sound and the shrine filling my visual field, as if sight and sound and self were all continuous, a larger organism than my body, with its interior and exterior parts working in synchronicity. Only the angles of the shadows on the shrine over the length of the day and the shifting color of the light marked the passage of time. There were moments when a ray of sunlight glancing off the golden ornaments sent a shiver through my whole body, or when the cool shift of evening's arrival surprised me with a stillness so profound, a suspension of breath and time so perfect, that joy welled up to fill the empty space.

Although Fujii Guruji had trained extensively in Zen as well as in other schools, he never taught the kind of meditation that Westerners have come to assume is essential to Buddhism. But the practice of drumming and chanting was as powerful a meditation as anything I learned later. It cleared a space in the mind where silence and stillness did their work naturally, unbidden.

I took the hand drum and walked outside, beating and chanting. There was a small votive stupa, three feet high, that served in place of the "unbuilt" one, and I circled it as I had learned to circle the stupa at Rajgir. Body in motion and voice loud, I spun a thread of loving devotion out of rhythm and repetition. The fact that the stupa was a miniature of what was envisioned on that spot seemed fortuitous, appropriate. The whole world thrummed with potential: a seed inside a fruit inside a flower, and a whole forest contained within that seed.

I walked into the woods, beating and chanting. Some mornings I went out before dawn, beating and chanting my way into the darkness. It didn't matter if I lost the path, I knew I could find my way back in daylight. All the noise I was making probably scared off any wildlife, but it didn't entirely account for the fearlessness that buoyed me. This single-minded focus was all I needed to be happy, all I would ever need. It was entirely sufficient. Nothing could ever take this from me. I was invincible.

At other times I would sit on the hilltop above the stupa's site for hours, taking in the silence. I watched the shadow of a cloud drift across the lake, the morning mist thinning in the valley, the gold blush on the Annapurnas turning a polished white. The peak of Machapuchare that faced me was like another stupa that Shiva had erected, its form echoing through the earth.

By this time I understood well what the mantra meant, the seven syllables *namu myoho renge kyo* honoring the Lotus Sutra. They were a summation in essence of all that the Buddha had taught. In that one phrase, the whole universe imploded into a single point. I could recite the sixteenth chapter of the sutra by heart, where the Buddha explains to his followers that leaving his father's palace on a quest for enlightenment and finally achieving it that night under the tree in Gaya was all an illusion created for their benefit: Enlightened beings only appear to come and go, making themselves available for a time in this faltering world, but in reality they are never gone. Enlightened beings are always present here and now if you truly yearn to see them.

Each time I read the sutra again, doors opened that I had passed by before. I pondered the Bodhisattva who makes an offering of his own body, the most precious of all possessions, by saturating himself with fragrant oils and setting himself on fire. That fire continued to blaze out across the universe for centuries, bringing light to as many worlds as there are grains of sand on the shores of eighty million Ganges. I had read in Fujii Guruji's autobiography about how he was inspired by this passage of the sutra to offer his own body, dedicating his physical existence entirely to the service of the Dharma. To seal that commitment he burned his flesh, a small token of the greater fire he felt, by tying a bundle of incense sticks to his arm and letting them burn all the way down. This made sense of the scars I had seen on both Okonogi and Nabatame. They must have done this exact same thing, I guessed, and I later learned that many monks in ancient China and Japan had done similar practices.

I resolved that I would do it too. I would make an offering of my body, this life's container that was so dear to me, the one possession that I would give up just about anything else to hold on to when danger threatened it. I would dedicate it totally, without reservation, to serve the Buddhas. *With one heart, single-minded, longing to see the Buddha.*

I tied the bundle of sticks to my arm, fumbling one-handed with the piece of string. I spoke my vow: From that time on, my body, speech, and mind were no longer my own. They belonged entirely to the Buddhas and my only purpose was service to the Dharma. With my entire being, I longed to see the world through open eyes. Then I began to chant slowly, steadily. I struck a match and set it to the incense. There was a feeling of deep familiarity, as if I had done this many times before. The smoke was heavy and sweet, and the burning sensation began, slowly at first and then very quickly. The smell of scorched flesh mixed with the smell of incense, and I had a flash—viscerally, through the core of this body that was no longer mine—of how thoroughly a cremation pyre would burn this flimsy, short-lived bundle of biochemistry to ashes. The pain faded—it was there, but it seemed distant, not troubling. A calm settled over me, steady as the slow measure of the chant. After a while I let go of the chant too. I sat cocooned in silence, the smoke twisting slowly in the air. Bright sunlight bleached the white walls and bounced off the gold ornaments of the shrine, and then in a sudden moment resolved into a dazzling brilliance that was infinitely more than reflections and sunlight. I was not alone. The space was filled with the presence of enlightened beings, resplendent with a multitude of Buddhas, each one of them witnessing this act. My offering was made, my commitment sealed.

When I got back to Lumbini a couple of weeks later, Nabatame noticed the wound, which was still pretty messy. Swimming in Lake Phewa before it healed had been a bad idea. He realized right away what I had done, and he was upset. "People can die from this kind of thing!" It was the only time I had seen his equilibrium falter. This was not something one did casually, or without guidance. Did I really understand its significance? he asked.

It's true that my understanding now is deeper than it was then. I've learned about the long tradition behind the rite that I instinctively improvised. I have learned too that there is a fine edge between detachment and neglect: If you dedicate your body to service, then part of the responsibility that entails is to preserve it from harm and keep it fit for service. But yes, when I decided to make an offering of my body that day, I wasn't playing. I understood very well the nature of the total commitment I was making.

Four years later and halfway around the world, I picked up the phone and heard the news that Nabatame had been assassinated. The workers were sleeping outside the huts to escape the summer heat when one woke up with a knife at his neck. Startled, he cried out and the intruder stabbed him with a warning to be silent. Nabatame woke at the cry and was shot in the head at close range when he got up. He died instantly. The workers who were woken counted six men, their faces masked, running off in the night.

Any facts beyond that remained murky. Nothing was stolen. The attackers spoke a local dialect but they were never identified. At first it was thought that the killing was related to a Hindu-Muslim altercation in the neighboring village that Nabatame had tried to mediate. Later, it was rumored that Nabatame was standing up against the corruption that trailed in the wake of a multimillion dollar UNESCO development plan to preserve Lumbini as a World Heritage site. The killers were said to be hired professionals.

The news of his death left me broken. I sat in my room reciting the sutra, pouring words into the vacuum that had been sucked out of me, and staring at the gifts Nabatame had given me when I first left Rajgir: the small Buddha statue and the hand drum with the mantra inscribed in Japanese characters that were at once delicate and bold. Anju-sama had told me that it was the drum that Fujii Guruji gave to Nabatame when he ordained him, and that the calligraphy was Fujii Guruji's own hand. I was stunned when I realized how precious that gift must have been to him, and I was humbled that he had given it so freely and kept its story to himself.

Nabatame loomed far larger in my mind than the brief and often silent time we had spent together. He was the first monk I ever met, and the gatekeeper of the world that opened to me at Rajgir. My memory of our days there and his quiet encouragement anchored my life in a time of profound uncertainty and upheaval. He was the one who gave me the precepts. Somehow, without thinking much about it, I had always assumed we would share a future: I would go back to Lumbini, we would work together again, there would be time to talk. I would no longer be a child and we would look back on those early days together. The story would continue. Only it wouldn't. I recognized there was a lesson here about change and grasping and impermanence, but I was blindsided by the feeling of absolute finality, the unassailable permanence of death in the midst of the world's flux.

I was shaken too when I understood that the monk who refused to kill snakes and scorpions to build the stupa was killed because of the stupa. The whole story may never see daylight, but I don't doubt that his death was the result of speaking truth to power. Nabatame moved through the world with a single-minded, uncompromising fearlessness—the same fearlessness that so many people who knew him well described of Fujii Guruji. I don't doubt that Nabatame learned it from his teacher. Nor was he the only one of Fujii Guruji's followers to die violently for standing on principle; another was killed in Sri Lanka in an almost gratuitous confrontation with the Tamil Tigers. Was the strange fearlessness I had felt walking in the forest before dawn, with the drum and chant lighting my way in the darkness, a small sip from that same spring? I wondered how Nabatame would have responded if he hadn't been surprised in his sleep. I don't think he would have fought back. Fujii Guruji believed that violence, even in self-defense, was an immoral response that we should learn to transcend. Should I honor this death? Was this an extreme instance of offering one's body in service, or was it a tragic waste of a precious life? The mind would sooner wrestle with a tangle of contradictions and seeming paradox than with the flat line of death.

The Nabatame that I so admired met everyone who crossed his path with a graceful acceptance that seemed to suspend judgment. I remembered the calm, evenhanded way he had handled the drama when Chacha-ji found me at Rajgir, sitting us down at the table to talk, guiding us to a resolution without taking sides. How is it possible to be single-minded and yet willing to listen to all sides of a story? To be uncompromising without being rigid?

There is a story told of the Marathi saint Jnaneshwar, who was bathing in the river and saw a scorpion struggling on the water. He picked it up to rescue it and return it to the shore, but the scorpion promptly stung his hand and the sudden pain caused him to shake the scorpion off. He tried again to pick it up, the scorpion stung him again, and the terrible pain once again caused him to drop it. This repeated many times before Jnaneshwar could finally get the scorpion safely to shore, where his disciple was watching in disbelief until he could no longer hold back. "Let the stupid scorpion drown!" he shouted. "It won't learn!" To which Jnaneshwar replied, "The poor scorpion is just following its nature: Its dharma is to sting. And I am following my dharma, which is to save creatures in distress."

Nabatame's uncompromising commitment to avoid harming others was his own kind and gentle dharma. He never expected gratitude and warmth from the scorpions and cobras he saved; he understood their nature. Perhaps if he better understood the nature of the hornet's nest he had somehow poked, he might still be alive today. We can learn to adjust our actions to avoid provoking a poisonous attack; we can learn to understand the nature of those who see us as enemies so we can navigate that reality more skillfully.

When the Bodhisattva Fukyo bowed to everyone who passed because they would one day become Buddhas, he bowed to his enemies too. If a snake had slithered by or a scorpion scuttled past in the dust, for sure he would have bowed deeply to them too. Each bow was an engagement, an expression of respect and faith in the possibility of change. If our enemies can change, if they aren't irredeemable, that change can only begin through engagement. How long it may take is beyond our knowing.

I have thought long and hard about the lessons embodied by Fujii Guruji and those like Nabatame who followed him closely. Like them, I dearly want to see a peaceful world, disarmament, and an end to war. I'm not convinced that the most effective way that I personally can move the world closer to that goal is by drumming and chanting. It seems more logical to work on diplomacy and negotiation between hostile parties, or designing policies to circumvent conflict, or educating human beings to see peace as a viable goal. And yet, who is to say that Fujii Guruji didn't affect many people profoundly, myself included, simply by walking the walk across continents on his path of absolute conviction and by building stupas like signposts to a more peaceful future? How else does one achieve a radical shift in human consciousness if not face-to-face, one by one, with deep affection and respect for each person one encounters on the way?

CHAPTER 8

Is There So Much Joy in Your Religion?

•
•
•

Are you looking for me? I am in the next seat.
My shoulder is against yours.
You will not find me in the stupas, not in Indian
  shrine rooms, nor in synagogues, nor in
  cathedrals:
not in masses, nor kirtans, not in legs winding
  around your own neck, nor in eating nothing
  but vegetables.
When you really look for me, you will see me
  instantly—
you will find me in the tiniest house of time.
Kabir says: Student, tell me, what is God?
He is the breath inside the breath.

—KABIR

"Did you think that all religious people were saints? Or that Buddhism is so pure that it has no place for politics?" My mother's words stung all the more painfully for the kernel of truth they contained.

The same summer that I traveled to Nepal, my father was transferred to New Delhi, which was the reason for the urgent phone messages from Okonogi calling me to return home quickly. The family's move toppled my precariously balanced life and I lost my safe haven at the temple in Kolkata. In Delhi, I was living with my parents once again and they took the opportunity to raise the temperature on their campaign to disabuse me of religion.

This time I had no escape. I had found my way to the small Japanese temple located near Gandhi's ashram in Delhi, but the welcome there was ambivalent. The nun in charge had been working for many years on a plan to build a stupa similar to the one at Rajgir, a complex and ambitious project that ran into constant bureaucratic obstacles in the capital. I was recruited to help with small tasks, moving paperwork through the system, which was not onerous in itself, but afforded me an uncomfortably close view of something I really didn't want to see.

There was another Japanese temple in the city, attended by a monk who had similar aspirations to build a stupa. The slow friction of their years-old competition was masked by Japanese politeness, but revealed itself in slights and snubs, in backhanded interventions and subtle jockeying for advantage. It demoralized me utterly.

It shook me profoundly to realize that monks and nuns could sink to jealousy, one-upmanship, and the confusion that seems to follow money like a hungry dog. Those I had come to know up to that point—whom I revered as elders and teachers—all seemed immune to provocation, skillful at deflecting trouble without avoiding it, unshakeable in their equanimity, poise, and patience. I knew that the hostility I was observing was wrong, but that very judgment sullied me too with disrespect for those I should have been able to look up to.

Saddest of all was the irony that this small-minded feud had attached itself to the building of a structure meant to symbolize the Buddha's mind: limitless, all-embracing, and unstained by such warped thinking. Again and again I asked myself: Was this so hard to figure out? They each wanted to build a stupa. Why couldn't they just work together?

The phone rang and my mother answered. "Khilari, it's for you." She covered the mouthpiece with her hand and whispered, "It's the nun from the temple."

I shook my head. "I'm not here."

In the tension that I couldn't hide, the sadness and avoidance, my mother sensed an opening and she probed it. "So you thought religion was above petty politics? You thought your monks and nuns were enlightened beings?" Where my father might lecture on the inevitable corruption of religious systems, the exploitation of the ignorant by the priesthood, and the opiate of the masses, my mother was direct and personal. "They brainwash you until you don't even see what they're doing. You lose touch with reality and believe their nonsense."

Our move to Delhi also meant that I was settling into a new high school at a critical time, coming up to the prelim exams to qualify for the national board exams the next year, and the ensuing cascade of college and career options. It was becoming clear that there would be no end to the forced march into the future that my parents had planned for me. When they weren't holding forth with rational historicism, or how so-and-so was making his mother happy with professional success, marriage, and grandchildren, they could infuriate me with pronouncements that were Brahmanical in their resistance to questioning. "You can't be ordained without our permission, so you'll just have to wait until our death."

The night before the exams were to start, the familiar arguments escalated into shouting and threats. "Why should I bother to sit for the prelims?" At the suggestion of passive resistance, my father's eyes grew big with fear, and he lashed back with his old threat to have the Japanese monks deported.

Hours later I was still in tears, sitting alone on the tiny balcony that I had claimed as my shrine. It was barely a room, walled with fiberglass sheets, attached to the apartment but not of it; but it held my statues, my photograph of Fujii Guruji, and my precious books. There was just enough room to sleep on the floor.

My father pushed open the door and sat on the floor beside me. We both faced the shrine, our backs to the wall, as if we needed some mediating force, not quite ready to face each other. In the dim glow that the city night diffused through the fiberglass, I could see that tears were streaming down his cheeks. So often I had seen him smolder and flare, or turn to silent stone, but I had never before seen him weeping. "I don't know what you want to do." His voice shook. "I would like to support you in your endeavors, but I cannot, you understand, because of the family's social status. And because I cannot, you are shortening my life."

Those words stayed with me through the night. They hung in the shuffling quiet of the exam hall and pushed my pen across the page for long hours. I was in two places at once, pulling answers out of some reluctant but automatic portion of memory, and standing on the edge of a deep hole, looking down into darkness. The whole point of Dharma was to bring an end to suffering. Yet everything I was doing was creating suffering for the people closest to me.

The temple offered no relief from home and home was no escape from the temple. It didn't matter which channel I turned to, there was a drama playing that wanted to suck me in. On each side I could see that the histrionics were unnecessary and unhelpful, the subplots were taking us in repeated circles, each and every one of the characters was creating their own misery and blaming it on someone else. I could see that it was all unreal—I was disillusioned in the truest sense of the word.

A few days after exams finished, I lay restless, unable to sleep. In the darkness a faint sound reached me and for a moment it silenced the pounding of my mind. It was music. Not the tinny blare of a transistor radio or a temple loudspeaker— these were unfiltered human voices, far enough away that the melody wouldn't have been audible over the traffic noise of daytime, but intermittently clear in the late-night lull. As if, through some luck of acoustics, clarity glanced off the back-alley walls, beckoning: *Come just a few steps closer.*

I got up, slipped out of the house in kurta and pajamas, and followed the sound through the shadowy alleys, the padlocked night face of the Karol Bagh neighborhood. Block by block it grew clearer, layered: the throb of a drum, a phrase repeated, voices conjoined, then one spiraling off. I stood in front of a large house, the upper story pulsing. The door was unlocked. The voices swept me in and up the staircase, into a high-ceilinged room that boomed with the praises of Krishna. Some forty people, men and women, were singing and dancing in a swaying sea of orange. I sat in a corner and let the chanting soothe me, relaxed into the ebbing, flowing unison. The rhythm of the mridangam accelerated in a brief frenzy, paused, signaled a shift. A lone voice began the familiar phrases of a Bengali devotional song, and the many voices echoed, the harmony swelling beneath them. Within moments I was carried off, swaying and singing, rising on the waves of sound.

I was flotsam and jetsam on a happy sea. My feet were pounding the rhythm, I was leaping from side to side, my arms flung wide, a simple bliss dragged out from some hiding place by the centrifugal force of the dance. The cymbals shook dust from my bones and my voice rose loud with the rest of the crowd.

How many hours was I bobbing, light and empty, on those waves of praise? Maybe four, five? It ended at the edge of dawn. I sat for a moment to catch my breath as the room was emptying, and a man who had caught my eye again and again in the swirling crowd came up to me. He was tiny, almost elfin, elderly by the evidence of his wrinkled face, but his bouncing endurance called that into question. His eyes glittered with glee under the bold V of the *tilaka* painted on his forehead, and he said to me: *"Tomar dharmo de eto anando pabajai ki?"*

The words were Bengali and I understood them: *Is there so much joy in your religion?* As I walked home through the alleys that were pink with dawn, feeling lighter than I had in months, the question turned over and over in my mind. The very asking, the very shape of the words on the tongue, seemed radiant with joy. The question took a grand somersault over the roof of circumstance—it was true that joy had abandoned my home and was conspicuously absent from the temples in Delhi. And yet here it was welling up inside me. Nothing had shifted on the horizon, and yet everything had shifted inside.

My parents were up already when I got home. I explained that I couldn't sleep and had gone for a walk. The mood at breakfast was oddly calm and easy, as if we had all simply exhaled and started afresh. I tried to nap for a while, but I was wide awake, electrified, brimming with energy.

Is there so much joy in your religion? The question spun me around. That beaming smile was an affirmation, a welcome, a knowing wink, but the question was also a gentle chiding. What had become of the joy, that most delicate tuning of the heart, that I encountered at Rajgir? My mind had turned brittle with ritual and righteous adherence to rules. Stubborn determination had been driving my practice for a long time. What was the point of religion if it was joyless and tiring? And where was this joy coming from now—not the kinetic discharge of the dance, releasing long-impacted tension, but the calm, clear feeling that lay underneath it? It was as if the music and dancing had popped the top off a bottle, and after the fizz had subsided I could see into it—there was no container at all, just a bottomless pool of light.

A teacher who could say so much with so little, who could crack open the world with a single question, was a teacher I needed to talk to. A question would be the beginning of a conversation. There would be more questions, and there would be someone to hear these groping intimations, and understand. I had to return to the temple and find him.

The alleys were transformed by the midday glare. Anticipation played tricks with distance as I retraced my steps uncertainly until the face of the house came into view, entirely familiar. The door was unlocked as it had been the night before. I slipped inside, blinded for a moment in the dim. The halls were silent, even as I could hear the song echoing in my mind. I walked up the stairs. Which door was it?

"Yes? You are looking for something?" He stood on the landing, had followed me up. Not a face I could remember singing, not one of the dancers.

"I was here last night. In the temple. At the *kirtan*."

"Not possible. There was no one here last night."

"But the temple is here?"

He opened the door as if in affirmation. Yes, this was the room, but empty. "We were not doing *kirtan* last night."

"There was a swami-ji. Very small. He was bald. He spoke Bengali."

"It is only me here today, no one else."

I scanned the room. There was no doubt: the statue of Krishna, deep blue and smiling in his niche, the faded orange bunting, the tile floor cool under my feet, the photographs . . . Hung high on the wall at the far side of the room were three framed portraits—photographs, though one, the largest, oldest, most imposing, was so retouched as to seem a drawing. But beside it was a fresher face, the eyes creased, as if with laughter, under a bald dome. "That's him!"

My guide look startled. He shook his head vigorously. "Not possible." His head kept shaking, as if he were trying to dislodge something from his ear. "Not possible."

"Where is swami-ji? I need to see him."

"Are you sure it was him? Not possible."

His repetition was exasperating.

"Yes, it was him. I want to talk to him."

"Maharaj-ji passed away five years ago."

I felt my hair stand up.

　　　　　　　　　　　*

I was right in my intuition that the mysterious Bengali's question about joy was the beginning of an important conversation, one that continues even today. It doesn't matter that he hasn't been present to hold up his half of the dialogue. I should have known by then that teachers come and go on their own schedule. From Fujii Guruji's first uncalled-for appearances to the anxious tedium of my long vigil with Shinozaki, I clearly wasn't in charge of the timetable and it wasn't my place to specify how a teacher should teach.

That simple question had taken me by surprise. Not only was joy absent from my life at that time, the possibility that there might be an essential bond between joy and religion had not entered my young mind. In my map of the world, the path that led to enlightenment traversed a terrain of vows and discipline and devotion. I had tasted joy, certainly, but it wasn't on the map. Something had just happened—invisible lines now popping into focus—which might not have happened if the swami had not appeared.

Meanwhile my interlocutor had vanished into thin air, as if to say, with that impish grin, "Forget about me! You have your question." I had only that single brief and ephemeral encounter with him, in the midst of an experience that was somehow unmoored from the physical world. My memory can barely reconstruct a visual image, but the sound of his voice remains perfectly vivid, and that lone question has served as a koan. In that sense the man I danced alongside that night was as truly a teacher as any other individual I have encountered.

Teachers don't come to us on our own terms. The teaching—what we need to learn—does not come to us on our terms. It's hardly an exaggeration to say that the entire Buddhist tradition, everything that has been passed down in lineage from teacher to student for two and a half millennia, is encapsulated in that. The whole point is that our preexisting notions are a voice crying from inside the distorted worldview that needs to be unlearned. As long as we insist that the lesson plan has to proceed according to our expectations, nothing a teacher says or does will make a difference.

The tradition remembers countless stories of students who endured tests of patience and fortitude to engage with a teacher. A student meditates for twelve long years to be rewarded, once, by a single visitation. Atisha sails from India to Sumatra to find his teacher, surviving storms, shipwrecks, and sea monsters. Marpa refused to teach Milarepa until he first built him a tower, stone by hand-hewn stone. Then Milarepa had to tear it down and rebuild it three more times at the teacher's whim. And the teacher refused to accept even that fourth and final construction—a tower so sturdy that it stands today, ten centuries later, as if in witness that this was no fairy tale—until Milarepa had hauled out its cornerstone from underneath it and replaced it with another.

It's easy to misplace the heart of these stories. If we read them as advertisements for the rarity and preciousness of what is to be gained—anything that demands so much effort must surely be worthwhile—we are applying a cost-benefit analysis in a domain where that logic is irrelevant, not to mention the deterrent of a bar set so high it seems the stuff of legend. The same calculation applies if we read Sisyphean endurance as a performance of devotion, proof that the student is worthy. We are bringing a transactional mindset to the spiritual project when we say that sacrifice is "rewarded," that the prize is "worthwhile," the student is "worthy." There is fallacy built into the very structure of habitual thought and the language we default to. As if there were some comparable scale of value by which one could weigh worldly patience against unworldly outcome. As if the bean-counting arbiter who keeps the ledger in the back of our mind were the final authority.

The whole point of the exercise is that we can't set the terms.

If we frame our terms in the language of psychology and read the student's submission to the teacher's demands as a protocol for breaking down the ego, it seems to make sense, but the translation is not entirely accurate. Western students who try to recreate a student-teacher relationship in the image of Eastern tradition too often misinterpret giving up control as giving up responsibility, as permission to regress. Far from dismantling the ego, the ego looms childishly large. Out come the shadow projections that reshape the entire idea of what a teacher is: the missing father, the parent to be pleased, the surrogate of all and everything. The transactional expectation, the quid pro quo, kicks in at a child's level: I'll submit, but only if you comfort and care for me. The student then values the relationship in proportion to access and proximity. Membership in the inner circle is the prize. Aside from the fact that the dynamic is ripe for abuse, it's ineffectual. Ego's voice undermines every experience, every interaction, demanding the comfort of belonging and identity. It's a setup for the kind of disappointment that will lead us to walk away from the half-built tower.

We're still dictating our terms, setting artificial conditions that sabotage the project. It never occurs to us that these terms could collapse. Indeed, they must collapse.

There is another lesson too, hidden in the teacher's absence, another very simple message embedded in the old stories of patient devotion, the uncomplaining eons that Milarepa spent moving stones from one spot to another. The muscles of self-

reliance grow stronger as the tower rises, while the surround-
ing fields are slowly cleared of stones. Patience isn't passive,
or it would never move us any closer to being ready. As long
as the teacher is unavailable, refusing to babysit or otherwise
follow the script of our expectations, we will have to figure
things out for ourselves. If we wait to be spoon-fed, we will go
hungry.

What if all this effort, the clearing of stones and the building of spiritual muscles, could somehow be done with joy? We
think of joy as the culmination of religious experience, but
perhaps joy is also a key to its cultivation.

When the student is ready, the teacher appears. The state-
ment is no less true for being apocryphal to the Buddhist
canon and comfortably at home on the Internet. Teachers
have a way of showing up when we are primed and ready to
learn. Traditionally, the turning point of renunciation is the
moment of readiness, and in the Buddhist universe renunciation is more or less synonymous with dis-illusion—the loss of
certain illusions about life. It's the moment when the terms we
have been clinging to collapse. Everything falls apart.

All that my parents ever wanted for me, all they longed for
with their loving hearts, was that I should flourish and be
happy. As far as they could see, I was determined to fail miserably at the business of flourishing and happiness. And my
own misery in the face of their resistance was no less loving
and generous than their misery. I really did want them to be
happy. After all, I had taken this great vow to make all sentient beings happy, to do my utmost to free them from suffering. And yet I was pounding my head against a wall; I not
only couldn't make Ma and Papa happy, it seemed I was hell-
bent on making them suffer.

Our disconnect was in the definition of happiness. The

happiness they were arguing for, and begging me to accept, was the notion of happiness that is contained entirely within the domain of conventional reality—not just the superficial happiness of sensory pleasures and material wealth, but also success, honor, earned recognition, a worthy legacy. The comforts of home and a relationship that embraces you for better or for worse. All the rainbow colors that cloak the illusion of security.

In some vague sense I understood this at the age of ten when I ran away. I had developed *vairagya,* the dispassionate detachment that turns away from conventional sources of happiness and self-validation, and recognizes pleasure as another category of suffering. I knew that pursuing a spiritual life meant turning my back on worldly concerns. I was standing at the gateway of renunciation, which is not a single threshold to be crossed but comes in stages. As we step gradually deeper into its stream, disillusion washes away both glitter and grime, not all at once but in layers.

I had become very heavily invested in renunciation. It was an essential part of who I was, an identity I was hanging on to for dear life. For four years I had soldiered against my parents' defenses, their ambushes and attacks, their vastly superior power to recruit spies and allies. I had somehow managed the most tenuous of victories, to live the life of a renunciant as I understood it, to make my home in any spiritual sanctum, from temples to charnel grounds, rather than in the bosom of family. The recognition that the life I had so idealized was as corrupt as anything else in this corrupted world came to me as the direst disillusion. My world was crumbling. In the words of a fourteen-year-old, everything I held dear was all "just another piece of crap."

When one reality comes tumbling down we conjure up another to fill its place as quickly as possible. We're grasping, one move to the next, hand over hand, but we don't ever let go of the rope. Here was the end of my rope. There was nothing left to grasp. I was in free fall. But somehow that strange *kirtan* in the night was a turning point. There was nothing left to grasp and I was fine with it. Into that opening, joy came rushing.

In America the narrative of renunciation is often linked to failure. When the market has crashed, when a marriage is betrayed, when the bottom falls out of denial, religion comes unbidden. With failure comes a surrender of the ego that has invested all its capital in the marks of mundane success, and from that ground-level view, renunciation holds the key to redemption. The spiritual life is a last resort.

In India, renunciation is traditionally seen as a last resort of a different kind, a retirement plan. In my parents' eyes I was upsetting the social and natural order by making religion a priority too early in life. "We are fully supportive of the spiritual life," they insisted, "but there is a right way to do this. A Brahmin should study for the first twenty-five years of life. The next fifty years are for doing productive work and providing for a family. Then, in your last twenty-five years, you can go live in the forest as a sannyasi and lead a spiritual life." (I could have argued that that rule excluded many of India's most prominent spiritual figures—Shankaracharya and Vivekananda both died in their thirties.)

Proximity to death powerfully evokes a last resort. Whether it's the prospect of the final curtain on a long life, or a startling brush with mortality at any time, death illuminates how illusory are the trappings of success, and rapidly realigns our values.

But what if renunciation calls to you not in the dregs of life but at the peak of possibility? The Buddha's own renunciation came at a time of wealth and flourishing, with a young family and a kingdom to inherit. Turning his back on all this is framed as a recognition of the fragility of human life and the suffering inherent in the human condition. But it also implies that enlightenment is genuinely possible, a viable endeavor, and deserves our best shot, not the diminished capacity of old age, illness, or depression. It implies that renunciation is worth a king's ransom, paid joyfully.

Can I even begin to describe the joy of spiritual disillusionment? The fact that it sounds like an oxymoron hints that language is vainly tossing a net into the ocean of the ineffable. *Kirtan* in essence means "praise" and although Krishna danced in the words that we sang that night and his flute reeled us, spinning, praise flowed from me without aim or boundary, not stopping at Krishna. It went beyond any object, a centrifugal force of love cast out to my entire world and beyond. But the center, the eye of this happy storm, was utterly calm. That sense of centered joy—still, poised, balanced— would stay with me for many days, weeks even, before it slowly receded, the wave washing back. If the ocean was no longer within view I knew its general direction: A stream inside me still flowed to it. Even if it would dry to a trickle in some seasons, that taste of joy remains available to memory.

I can say what it's not. It's not just another rung on the ladder of sensory pleasure and conventional notions of happiness. It's not eudaemonia, that pinnacle of human flourishing that the Greeks debated, and it's not the apex of Maslow's hierarchy. There are Buddhist commentaries that analyze fine gradations of joy at the edge of imagining that may seem far beyond any relevance to our lives, distinctions of bliss and great bliss and ultimate bliss. The tradition also warns us in no uncertain terms that joy is not the goal, and if we make it the focus of our efforts, it becomes a distraction and a trap. It's not to be sought. It arises only when you're not chasing it.

The joy of disillusion tastes like freedom. It has overtones of fearlessness, and an absence of impurities—bias of any kind—that might cloud its clarity. And yet it's not remotely uncaring, indifferent, or in any way sociopathic. Its disillusion is a disenchantment, which is only to say that some spell of illusion has been broken. It doesn't look unkindly on those who remain in the bonds of that spell. On the contrary, it's deeply compassionate. The Bodhisattva returns voluntarily, again and again, into the world of suffering to offer whatever relief is possible. The capacity to do that requires a lifeline to an infinite storehouse of joy. Indeed, perfecting the practice of joyful effort is one of the "perfections" that defines the path of a Bodhisattva. How else to meet infinite suffering face-to-face and not be defeated?

Indeed, the joy of disillusion is so profoundly connected to the human condition that it spills contagiously on anyone with whom it comes in contact. Our psychology is exquisitely sensitive to this overflowing joy. I have been blessed to meet individuals who seem to live in that state much of the time, who sustain it without exhaustion, and whose joy is effervescent, radiant, and uncontainable. A few moments spent in their presence leaves an unmistakable trace. Every one of them has been a teacher. Not every one has shared a lesson that was articulated in words, not even in a cryptic question. Sometimes the mere presence of a powerful model is all the lesson that's needed.

•

So the Bengali swami dropped his question on me and disappeared. Perhaps he had urgent business elsewhere, other seeds he needed to plant while the earth was freshly plowed. There was an irony in this strange encounter that was not lost on me. After chasing dreams and teachers across the subcontinent and into the Himalayas, navigating railways, bus lines, and border crossings by horse cart, immersing myself in the language of medieval Japan—all of this far-flung quest was brought up short on my home turf, a few blocks from my parents' very ordinary civil service apartment near the noisy markets of Karol Bagh, with the simplest of questions posed by a figure who, if oddly ephemeral, was of our homegrown faith. I wasn't inclined to interpret it literally, abandon Buddhism and settle into my parents' life plan. Instead, in the spirit of a monk's commitment to homelessness, I took it as a metaphor for self-reliance. I would have to trust in my own discernment.

In any case, I had my assignment: *Is there so much joy in your religion?* I would continue to ponder his question for years to come, but in all the myriad reflections, the many facets that have shone at different times, one answer is consistently clear. Joy lies at the very heart of spiritual practice. We would be wise, therefore, not to invite misery into this realm. There is no place here for pious demonstrations of imperviousness to pain. There is no purpose to self-inflicted martyrdom. There are so many avenues, so many places for suffering, let religion not be one of them. Its only purpose is the end of suffering.

CHAPTER 9

Turning of the Wheel and the Mind

.
.
.

Should you find a wise critic to point out your
faults, follow him as you would a guide to
hidden treasure.

—BUDDHA: DHAMMAPADA

Sometimes a jewel can lie right under your nose for years before it catches the light at a particular angle and you finally
see its brilliance.

The first time I met Reverend Sasaki, I was around twelve,
still living in Kolkata. I had told my parents that I wanted to
go to the holy city of Varanasi to pay my respects to the Ganges. Perhaps they felt a glimmer of hope that I was showing
interest in my Brahmin roots rather than Buddhism, or perhaps they were just tired of arguing, but they let me go.

Is a pilgrimage that's hidden under a veil of pretense any
less of a pilgrimage? When I reached Varanasi I didn't wander
in the dark lanes of India's most sacred, ancient, shining city,
or linger on the steps descending into the slow drift of Mother
Ganga's expansive embrace. Just a few kilometers farther, at a

quiet and green remove, was my real destination—Sarnath. This was the place where the Buddha first taught, and it still holds a deep power, as if an elephant's footsteps reverberate through the earth many centuries after it walked this ground.

The words that the Buddha spoke there are said to have set a wheel turning that would continue in motion at Sarnath, at Rajgir, at Vaishali, and far beyond. Those words would be remembered, repeated, expounded, and they still echo now, two and a half millennia later. That wheel left a deep impression in India's soil and even marks the flag of its rebirth as a secular state since Independence. Sarnath was the site not only of the Buddha's first teaching but also of the first retreat, the quiet season of meditation during the monsoon rains. When the rain ended and the roads were passable, it was the center from which the Buddha first sent monks out to travel homeless in the world, embodying what they had learned and making themselves available to others.

Sarnath remains the still center of the turning wheel and it drew a young Sasaki into its axis, much as Fujii Guruji was drawn to Rajgir before him, both of them spurred by Nichiren's prophecy that Buddhism would return to India from Japan and be revived there after dying out. Though Sasaki went back to Japan for regular visits, his roots had dug deep into the soil of Sarnath. Nothing that life in India could throw his way ever shook his resolve to stay, not even several near-death bouts with illness.

When I first showed up at the Horinji temple in Sarnath, I knew nothing about this monk or how he had built the temple slowly, through decades of determination. I was surprised that his face lit up when he saw me. "Somebody came here searching for you a while ago." He showed me a small, dog-eared, black-and-white photo of myself—the photo my father had distributed to temples and mosques and shrines in his dragnet across India when I ran away. We laughed together at that slightly younger me, and I felt oddly welcome.

We met again on several occasions, at Rajgir, at the temple in Kolkata, and in Delhi. Though the Japanese monks in India were from different schools, their paths crossed often, and on those paths, Sasaki's reputation preceded him. He belonged to the Nichiren Shu school, the "mother ship" that Fujii Guruji had sailed from, and he was known as something of a rebel, simultaneously esteemed by and at odds with the establishment back in Japan. He expressed strong opinions about how monks in Japan had been reduced to functionaries in the funeral business; how that was demeaning and not what Buddhist monks should be doing with their lives. His compatriots in India got a more tongue-in-cheek critique. "These monks are too lazy," he would say, dismissing them as well as his own verdict on them with a laugh. "Just come to Sarnath." With that he would finish off his glass, bottoms up. It wasn't unusual for Japanese monks to drink alcohol, unlike Buddhist orders elsewhere. Even so, Sasaki was legendary. I often heard him joke that he was the Old Monk who gave India's most popular brand of rum its name. Then he would light yet another cigarette and puff away, adding to the very effective smoke screen with which he surrounded himself. He worked very hard at not having followers.

By the time I got to know Sasaki, I had already become a zealous perfectionist in the matter of monastic vows. The fact that I wanted so badly to be ordained, and fought so bitterly for it against my parents, made me fiercely determined to keep the vows in all respects as if I really were a monk. I had discovered the Vinaya, the text that explains the very detailed rules governing the conduct of monastic life. I had met monks from

Sri Lanka and Burma, whose discipline was an inspiration to me. For them the rules of the Vinaya were still vital in a way that had largely faded from memory in Japanese Buddhism. I decided, like a good monk, that I would not eat after the midday meal, which my mother took as the worst possible offense of Buddhism against the health of a growing boy, and I lost that battle after a couple of months. But my righteous adolescent self remained quick to judge the discipline of every monk I encountered, and Sasaki was not excluded from that exercise.

The lesson that I needed to learn in all this was one that Sasaki held in reserve. He would wait until I returned to Sarnath after a long detour to Syracuse, New York.

It had become perfectly clear that my parents would never back down: Over their dead bodies would I become a fully ordained monk. I was caught in the gears of a machine that was manufacturing my future, step by incremental step. In desperation, I threw a spanner in the works. I decided to fail the national board exams that controlled the fate—the eligibility for college—of every high school student in India.

Day after day I sat in the exam room. I wrote my name and number on each paper, sat quietly until the end of the session, and handed in the blank papers. I was not going to walk out early and merely get disqualified. No, I was determined to fail, unequivocally, irrevocably, and without remedy. Word got out. My silent protest was the talk of the school. When my parents learned, they were in shock; they refused even to believe the story until they saw those big zeros. Their fury then was tempered by the sadness of genuine loss. I had indeed thrown away my future. Any possible damage control was now severely circumscribed by those zeros, but they swung into action regardless. I would be packed off to live with my uncle's family in the suburbs of Syracuse, New York, airlifted to safety beyond the reach of the Japanese monks' mind control and India's too-pervasive fog of spirituality. They found a school in Syracuse with an international exchange program that accepted me.

I didn't want to leave, and it was only Anju-sama's blessing that finally got me out the door. Education was never a bad thing, she insisted. It was what her own son had lacked, and she wished she had been able to provide better for him. My father and my grandfather saw me off at the airport. All around us, families were saying goodbye to departing students with a familiar script: *Study hard! Don't go to clubs, don't party, stay away from alcohol! Just study, focus on your studies* . . . My grandfather gave me a big hug, and said, "Enjoy yourself. If you find a girl, send me a picture."

On the flight, thirty thousand feet above nowhere, I made a decision, late as it was, to stop making my parents miserable. The only way I could see to do that was to give up my practice—no more meditation, no more prayers—and turn my back on the spiritual life. I would fill the hole that was left by studying hard.

And so I entered into a time of strangeness that sticks in memory as an extended bad dream, a cultural disorientation compounded by a spiritual one. I struggled earnestly to blend in, but like any kid fresh off the boat, I stumbled on the rocks on shore: My courtesy offended the female teachers' gender politics. I was spooked by American teenagers' mating rituals—did going on a date mean you had to get married? I acquired the nickname PD because Priyadarshi was unpronounceable. There were pleasant moments—I enjoyed playing soccer and DJ'ing for parties—but ultimately it all seemed a pointless charade and my participation was forced, acted out in obligation.

After four months, my body joined forces with my mind in full-on rebellion. I felt sick, and couldn't muster the effort to talk to people. Food sat heavy in me and refused to digest. One morning I woke up in a worse state than ever, and instinctively I sat to meditate and do some prayers. I felt like I had just been given oxygen and could breathe freely for the first time in many weeks. A drink of cool water in the desert, a freshness that people commented on repeatedly that day. It was obvious that trying to stop was a mistake. I would have to figure out how to integrate practice into this life that my parents had conjured up to cure me. Discreetly, quietly—no loud drumming—I set aside time each morning and evening in my room.

I did well at school, but going home when I graduated wasn't an option. Much as I missed India, I refused to return to the domain where my parents had total control. I went through the motions of applying to college and collected a stack of Ivy League acceptances that would have thrilled my parents if only they knew. I didn't tell them. I was determined not to accept their financial help, but my student visa didn't allow me to get a job. I was stuck in a stubborn bind until a scholarship to Le Moyne College in Syracuse rescued me.

The Jesuit brothers of Le Moyne also provided a balm for my deeper problem. No one there was going to argue that the spiritual dimensions of life were not a worthy priority. I finally felt at home. I found my footing in the international students' organization, in interreligious dialogue and the philosophy symposium. I studied Christian texts with the Jesuits and argued Jewish philosophy with my advisor Rabbi Michael Kagan, who was very dear to me. In fact, I was doing so well that I was on track to graduate early, which was a problem, given my student visa and uncertainty about next steps.

Rabbi Kagan suggested that I could solve the problem by declaring additional majors and taking a year to study abroad. Never mind that I was already "abroad"—I realized that it meant I could go home to India for a year on my own terms, to reconnect with old teachers and seek out new ones. I could continue studying Buddhism, and because it was all part of the university's program, my parents could not object. Father Ryan found a grant to cover airfare, a laptop, and a camera—I would have to report on my experience—and I knew I could stay at monasteries and live on almost nothing.

After a few days in Delhi, in the limbo of reentry, I was on my way to Sarnath where I had an invitation to study at the Central Institute of Higher Tibetan Studies. This brought me back to Sasaki. I figured I could stay at his temple, at least until I got my bearings.

Somehow, in the confusion of boarding the train in Delhi—passengers matching tickets to seats and stowing luggage and families squeezing in—my daypack disappeared even before the train pulled out of the station. With it went the new laptop, the camera, and all the cash I had on me, enough to cover the months of my stay. The ten-hour ride was time enough to defuse the surge of anger aimed both at the thief and my own carelessness. By the time the train pulled into the station at Varanasi, I had settled into acceptance, but I still needed to get to Sarnath somehow without bus fare.

Once when the Buddha traveled to Sarnath, the story goes, he had no money to pay for the ferry across the Ganges. Instead he simply vanished in front of the startled boatman's eyes and reappeared on the far bank. When news of this event reached the king, he granted free passage on the ferry to all monks, but somewhere in the labyrinth of history that custom had lapsed. I took a cab. It was more expensive than the bus, but that way I could ask Sasaki for help with the fare when I got there.

When we reached the temple and I knocked at his room, the Venerable Sasaki didn't disappoint. The door opened on a familiar sight—those baggy pajamas, a towel draped over his head, and a cigarette dangling. "Traveling light?" he asked, as a big smile spread across his face. "Don't worry, you can stay here. I'll cover your expenses." Any words I had ready were knocked right out of me. All I could do was laugh.

Sasaki let me use one of the old computers in the office in place of my stolen laptop and shared his Yamaha 160 so I could ride to classes in Sarnath and Varanasi. I settled into what was perhaps the happiest period of my life. A banquet was laid out before me, and I was hungry. I dove headfirst into the Nalanda masters, guided by scholars with a lifetime's knowledge of Buddhist philosophy. I studied Tibetan, and I sat with pandits who taught Sanskrit orally in the traditional manner—it flowed easily for me and unlocked memories of summers spent reading Sanskrit poetry with my grandparents. I met young monks who were not so unlike myself, made friends from Ladakh and Tibet and began to learn about varieties of Buddhism that were different in so many particulars from the Japanese I had grown up with, though we all shared this heartland at Sarnath. There were whole libraries at my disposal and great minds open for the asking. It was a feast where each dish offered deep nourishment, a season's bounty bursting fresh in my mind, and the complex flavors of long tradition.

Sasaki observed my voracious learning binge with a certain skeptical reserve. He had always drawn a bright line between textual interpretation and in-the-flesh realization. There were scholars and there were practitioners, and I knew which was the real deal in his mind. Sasaki himself never taught. There was nothing to teach, he said. Those who wanted to learn would come, and they would learn what they would learn. "If Sasaki teaches," he would say, "they learn what Sasaki says. They don't learn what Buddha says. Sasaki cannot teach like Buddha."

So I was more than a little surprised when he summoned me from my room to talk to a group of visitors at the temple. "They're here to learn about Buddha Dharma," he said. "Teach them." Some were Indian, some Japanese, not monks but pilgrims, or tourists with a more than superficial interest. I was nervous and entirely unprepared for this test; I dreaded the critique that was sure to follow. I tried to join the guests sitting on the ground, instinctively aiming for the leveling effect of an American classroom circle. "No!" Sasaki planted a chair and made me sit above them. "Teaching Dharma you have to sit there," he insisted. He took a seat at the back of the room and glared at me steadily.

Just begin. May it somehow be helpful. Begin at the beginning. "You're in Sarnath," I said. "This is the place where Buddhism began, where the Buddha first taught."

How could I possibly imagine what it was like the first time that the Buddha shared what he had seen that night under the Bodhi tree? Having arrived, the whole of the path he had traveled was visible to him. Where the path ended was where suffering ended. It took weeks before he could even begin to think that it was possible to communicate what he had learned. He walked the hundred and fifty miles from Bodhgaya to Sarnath, to the Deer Park where his five friends who had been comrades on the path were still searching for what he had found. Those five friends would become the first monks. De facto, no rules or ordination; the Buddha's own presence and example were guide enough. What he had learned could indeed be taught.

I can't remember what words I found that day, only that I did my best to echo that first teaching, to add my small voice to the centuries of echoes and offer a tiny nudge to help keep the wheel turning. The heart of the Buddha's first lesson that he shared with his friends is summarized in four points, mnemonically enshrined as the Four Noble Truths. The first describes the world as we know it, the truth that all of our existence is painful: Not just the slings and arrows that the universe aims our way and the harm we do to one another, but also how loss is ever-present in an impermanent world and how it shadows even our fleeting moments of happiness. The second truth reveals the causes of that suffering: ignorance and grasping. How we cling to everything we touch— the people, the possessions, the circumstances that we believe will make us happy—and remain ignorant of a deeper source of happiness that will outlast anything we could grasp. The third truth is that this constant escalation of suffering, though natural and normal, is not eternal or necessary. The Buddha taught that it is possible to free ourselves from this suffering, and the fourth truth is the path to that liberation, which involves practicing ethical conduct, the mental discipline of meditation and mindfulness, and the wisdom that erases the illusions of ignorance, recognizing that there is nothing to grasp or cling to that stands apart from the flux of perpetual change and interrelationship.

Sasaki seemed to have dozed off. Then one eye opened, and I knew he was wide awake and had heard every word. When the visitors wandered off, he steered me out of the temple and we walked to a nearby tea shop. *Now the critique begins,* I thought. He gave some change to the chai wallah and told him to go buy cookies. When the box arrived, he opened it with all the excitement of a little kid opening a present, and offered me a celebratory cookie. "I'm impressed," he said. "You're learning well." The cookie was nice. Buttery. And then gone. The praise felt good. Sort of like the cookie, buttery and then gone.

•

While I was staying with Sasaki at the temple in Sarnath, my father came to visit. He said he had business in Varanasi but clearly he was making an effort to reach out to me. Sasaki insisted that he stay with us and fussed over fixing up a room for him. He seemed as excited in anticipation of the visit as I was apprehensive.

In the end it went smoothly, because both elders found a certain common ground. My father discovered that Sasaki had a wife. She was a nun who lived in Japan and looked after their home temple. This was not at all unusual in Japan, however unthinkable in the Buddhism of other traditions. During the Meiji Restoration in the nineteenth century, celibate monks without possessions or worldly obligations were seen as a threat to the state, much as the samurai were. You can't control someone who has nothing to lose. So monks were pressured to marry, temples became property that was passed on through inheritance, and monastic ordination evolved into a hereditary priesthood. Fujii Guruji's return to a stricter vision of monastic discipline that included celibacy was exceptional in the world he was born into.

When my father discovered that monks in Sasaki's school could marry, a light bulb switched on: Here was a win-win solution to our intractable conflict. Obviously, I should be ordained as a Nichiren Shu monk, just like Sasaki, who thought it was a great idea. To me it seemed pointless and irresponsible. You couldn't very well support a family and live in the world without ignoring a huge portion of how the Buddha had taught that a monk was supposed to live. You would either be a monk in name only, or a poor excuse for a husband. Neither fish nor fowl. My father clung to the idea until his dying day, but Sasaki conceded the common sense of my position: "So the monk now lives in India and the wife lives in Japan. What's the point?"

"It's true, there is no point!" he laughed.

It was this open-minded, nonjudgmental embrace of circumstance that made me feel bold enough to ask Sasaki for guidance on a related question that had gnawed at me for a long time. It was the issue of women. Not the ordinary question of women as most young men might define it, nor even the annoyance of my parents' obsession with marriage and procreation, but the delicate issue of women and vows, and the seemingly contradictory messages built into the tradition. The prescriptions of the Vinaya are very specific about avoiding contact with women, avoiding even the appearance of impropriety. If I lived in a monastery, no doubt the logistical challenges would be moot, but it seemed impossible to negotiate the physical space of the modern world, the classrooms and dormitories and elevators and crowded buses, without breaking the rules.

At Le Moyne, I lived at Father Daniel Berrigan's International House, which at that time shared the building with a Latino frat house. My neighbors came from the Dominican Republic, Puerto Rico, and the Bronx. They partied late and had girlfriends who spent the night. Our first wary encounters warmed into a respectful if oddly matched friendship. They could count on my prayer bells to get them out the door just in time for class in the morning, and they welcomed my tutoring in math and science. They made a conscious effort not to swear in front of me, as if I were a Catholic priest, and they warned me in advance if the movie they were watching that night wasn't suitable. But to the girls I was a challenge. Insistent efforts to teach me to dance salsa—"hold me tighter, PD, like this!"—made me blush, to the loud applause of all present.

It wasn't really my own feelings that defined the opposite sex as a problem. I may have been naïve compared to Americans my age, but I wasn't fantasizing about where the dancing might lead or running Bollywood romances in my head. My feelings were neutral, but the texts I was studying were not. From the earliest beginnings of Buddhist monasticism, women were seen as distractions to practice. A monk should control his thoughts. A monk should not be alone with a woman in a vehicle, in a room, in a secluded place. A monk should keep his eyes cast down.

There were practices designed to subdue desire and tame attraction, and I took them on diligently. I had visited the charnel grounds in Varanasi and sat on the ghats as the light faded in the evening, watching the corpses burning atop piles of wood. The sputtering, steaming, twisting, crackling reality of a once-human body, "a sack of pus, blood, and bone," now fueled the flames. Nothing attractive there. I looked at people on the street and visualized them as skeletons. Men too, but women especially. That hand raised to steady a bundle on her head, the angle of a shoulder, those legs side-saddle on the back of that motorcycle—all were reduced to the minimal architecture of bleached bone. I erased the bare skin, the gleaming hair, the curve of a lip, the colorful swirl of clothing. With my x-ray vision and a harsh dose of impermanence, I defeated the forces of attraction. No, there's nothing beautiful here at all, nothing more than what will remain when the drama of death's decay has slowed to a microscopic crawl.

But other texts that I was studying, and my own common sense, turned that thinking upside down. This whole project of enlightenment wasn't just about me. Women were sentient beings too, and not just objects of attraction. I should be training myself to feel lovingkindness and compassion for all beings equally, not reducing them to a fraction of their reality or a figment of my imagination. I didn't have to look further than my own family to know that women—young or old, educated or otherwise—were every bit as formidable and deserving of respect as any man. Whether or not I saw them as attractive had nothing to do with it.

This was the conundrum that I hoped Sasaki could help me untangle. As difficult as it was to ask, I could trust that my question would not be met with ridicule or embarrassment. I told him I needed to talk to him and he set aside time that same evening.

Sasaki was waiting for me in his room. He sat with a pot of green tea, two glasses, and a bottle of Johnny Walker set out in front of him. He poured a little whisky in each of the glasses, pushed one toward me, and took a sip of his own. This was a new twist. Though his habit was infamous, he had never offered me a drink before, and I was dumbfounded. I sat still, said nothing, but in my head I was yelling, *No way! You must be crazy to think I would touch that stuff.*

He finished his glass slowly, savoring it. He poured himself another. Long minutes went by in silence, maybe half an hour with only the faintest sound of a car in the distance, a fly buzzing. Finally he asked, "Aren't you going to drink?"

"I can't drink. It's against my vows."

"Oh, I forgot about those." He said it so disingenuously I

could half believe he was not actually mocking me. "Well, you said you wanted to have a conversation. I don't converse with people who don't drink."

This is ridiculous, I thought. *Should I just forget about asking for advice?* I decided to wait a bit longer, hoping he would drop it. Another quarter of an hour passed. It wasn't as if we couldn't both sit silently all night.

Finally he spoke. "Would you like some green tea in your whisky?" I had never heard of such a thing, but I figured he was making an effort to compromise and I should meet him halfway.

"All right," I conceded. He poured and I took a sip. The burning sensation was strange to me.

"These vows of yours, what are they good for?" I was startled by the harshness in his voice. He normally spoke very gently unless something really upset him. I gave the standard answers as I'd learned them. The vows protect one's practice. They prevent distractions and wrong turns and keep you focused on the path to enlightenment.

"And what is the purpose of enlightenment?"

"To benefit sentient beings . . ."

"So do your vows benefit sentient beings? How exactly does that work?"

I groped for an answer. "If I get rid of ego . . ."

"And these vows—are they helping you to get rid of your ego?"

That landed a blow. I defended without thinking. "In some ways."

"In what ways?" My mind went blank. He pushed on. "Aren't your vows inflating your ego? Aren't they obscuring your view of everyone and everything around you? How can you help sentient beings if you feel superior to them? How

can you let go of your ego when you feel superior to everybody here?"

The feeling of something shattering inside me was physical.
A cracking sound, loud, hard, and brittle.

"Have another sip." I didn't argue. I drank the burning
liquid. "Of all pride, the most dangerous is spiritual pride. It's
the blind spot that leads to one's downfall. So make up your
mind if you want to be a Bodhisattva and benefit others. Or
else"—and here the nonjudgmental Sasaki returned with a
shrug—"just practice well for your own benefit."

And so, with all that as preface, and from a much more
humble position than when I had entered his room, I was finally able to ask Sasaki my question. To be fair, with his typical prescience he had already given me an answer. But still I
asked, struggling to choose my words without falling into the
whirlpool that circled in my own mind. Having dragged the
question around since high school, and up and down the halls
of Le Moyne, it seemed complicated, a story with an endless
cast of characters, each with their own backstory, foot-
notes . . .

His answer was a simple, straight blade that cut through all
my circuitous ifs, ands, or buts: "If you're too attached to
your vows, you'll be blinded by all kinds of discrimination,"
he said slowly, and then continued as if the choice were evenhanded: "If you're not so attached to your vows, you won't
see men and women. Instead you'll see Buddhas."

Not men, not women, but human beings. And every human
being that stood before me was a potential Buddha, infinitely
worthy of love and respect. There was the Bodhisattva Fukyo
standing at the gate, bowing in deepest reverence to every
man and woman, every dog, every donkey.

Sleep didn't come that night. I lay awake in the dark for

hours, pondering our conversation. I poked gently at the wound that had opened, not wanting to bandage it quickly or minimize the effect. I could recognize that the sting of shame was not something to pull back from; these were growing pains.

Spiritual pride is the blind spot that leads to one's downfall.

I knew what spiritual pride was, or so I thought. I had seen plenty of priests acting like politicians, concerning themselves with who had the bigger following, who sat on the higher throne, who built the bigger temple. That kind of pride was the very antithesis of the humility that every spiritual tradition honors. It was so clearly grasping, treasuring oneself, clinging to an illusion of identity. Buddhism 101, Noble Truth number two, the root cause of suffering. That wasn't me. But the self-righteousness, the stance of moral superiority that Sasaki had recognized—that was spiritual pride too, of a more subtle form.

Our blind spots are often surrounded by bright neon arrows pointing straight at them, flashing brazenly. Not only was my fierce attachment to a lofty goal still a fierce attachment, but my whole story—the who-what-where-how-and-why of me, my endless conflict with my family, my future always just out of reach, my very purpose in life—was woven out of tight bands of that same attachment. Behind all the longing, all the devotion, all the pure-minded determination to do it right, there stood a boy with both arms wrapped tightly around himself. And if that wasn't bad enough, he had his Brahmin nose held high, looking down on everyone else.

What exactly were these vows that my ego was so invested in? The more than two hundred vows compiled in the Vinaya texts (the exact numbers vary in different traditions) were rules to guide the early monastic community. In essence, they guard against doing harm, including the myriad ways that ethical failures might harm the cohesion of the community, or its relationships with the outside world, or a monk's progress on the path. Ethics shade into etiquette and deportment— how a monk conducts himself in all circumstances. Although the rules are detailed and comprehensive, their spirit is far from absolute. They come with accounts that explain how they were devised to resolve particular conflicts or perceived transgressions that had arisen in the daily life of the monks who followed the Buddha during his lifetime, and so they are embedded in the culture of their historical moment. The Buddha emphasized again and again that their spirit mattered more than their letter, and at his death he said that the minor rules could be abandoned as times changed.

But the monks could not remember with certainty which rules were categorized as minor, and so they kept them all. In the Theravada schools that prevail in Southeast Asia, and have continued in a line unbroken since the Buddha's lifetime, the rules are recited regularly and are absolutely central to monastic life. The discipline of monitoring one's own adherence is a core practice that both demands and hones a constant awareness. Living in such a constrained manner requires deep discipline, determined motivation, and constant mindfulness. It is those very factors of discipline, motivation, and mindfulness that will eventually do the work of transformation.

Though the monastic vows emerged from and are entirely enmeshed in communal life, they are individual commitments. They are most emphatically not a competitive sport. The kind of comparisons and score-keeping that hooked my adolescent mind instantly defeats their purpose. But it's no surprise that we drag old habits of mind along with us onto the spiritual path. The longing to belong, the instinct to discriminate, the enthusiasm that gropes for a way to express itself and finds its form in pride—these urges don't disappear overnight just because we discover that we have spiritual aspirations. In my yearning for the certainty and identity that ordination seemed to promise, even in the absence of any real monastic community, I had latched on to one of the most pervasive problems of monastic life.

My holier-than-thou judgment was not peculiarly mine. Self-righteous spiritual pride drives the sectarianism that plagues organized religion, and Buddhism is no exception. It might begin innocently, when the eagerness and joy generated by your own practice, your own progress, or the presence of your own teacher, express themselves in superlatives. Eventually those superlatives come to imply the denigration of all others. There is only one "best" and everything else is therefore inferior. Group dynamics—the team spirit of my monastery versus yours—compound the problem. Sasaki often talked about "the ego of institutions" that had caused the historical divisions of lineages, the proliferation of countless schools as Buddhism spread across Asia, each branch splitting off multiple times, some withering, some thriving, growing into great limbs or dividing into further branches, right down to the tiny twig that was Fujii Guruji's small group.

So make up your mind if you want to be a Bodhisattva and benefit others. Or else . . . just practice well for your own benefit. Hidden in that evenhanded shrug of equivocation was a finger pointing at what was, by some accounts, the biggest split of all, dividing Buddhism into two streams across the continent of Asia, and separating the Mahayana schools that became dominant in China, Tibet, and Japan from the older tradition that is still very much alive in Myanmar, Sri Lanka, Cambodia, and Thailand.

In the stream that flowed north, an expansive vision opened, beyond the historical record of one great teacher's life and legacy, onto a cosmology permeated by the potential for enlightenment. Its driving energy is the altruistic motivation of the Bodhisattvas. It takes as its aspirational models such figures as Avalokiteshvara, protector and guardian, the embodiment of compassion, who hears the cries of suffering sentient beings and takes on whatever form will relieve them. It recognizes the impossible scale of the task without faltering. After countless eons of reaching out in aid, Avalokiteshvara surveyed his work and saw there was still endless need. At the sight of so much pain, he shed a single tear, and from that tear was born Tara, the feminine Bodhisattva of compassion-in-action, swift and effective, saying, *I will help; I will be your companion in this work.* A Bodhisattva's life is bound by a deceptively simple intention: to place others before yourself on the path to enlightenment. The radical humility of that intention should serve as an antidote to spiritual pride. If you have boundless aspirations for the welfare of all sentient beings, you won't get the job done by sitting atop a mountain of righteous virtue, looking down on them as spiritually inferior.

And if you weren't moved to aspire to that impossibly vast embrace of all beings, then, as Sasaki said, just practice well for your own benefit, and aim to get yourself enlightened. Though I knew well enough in which stream he swam, the even-tempered simplicity of his pronouncement truly carried no shade of judgment. But if you did choose that older, narrower path, he implied, you wouldn't get far by using your vows as bricks in a wall to defend your inflated self-image.

Ultimately that either-or choice was an illusion, two sides of the same coin that flipped on whether you fix yourself first, or throw yourself from the beginning into the project of fixing the world. In truth, you can't do one without doing some of the other. You'll never have the skill and the emotional resources to save the world without first developing a certain level of self-knowledge, forbearance, focus, and ethical discipline—in other words, a certain level of spiritual maturity in your own life. And likewise, you'll never reach that maturity without a simultaneous investment of compassion and openhearted awareness of your kinship with the flawed and needy world. They are one and the same reality, circling each other, and the difference is only a matter of where you begin to tell the story. Sasaki wasn't going to preach that one choice was better than the other. But whichever side you choose, he was saying, do it right.

Shame is a powerful, if bitter, medicine. My fault was exposed, and that exposure gave rise to a newly reflective awareness. My remorse was genuine. The way to put it right was to study how to avoid repeating the offense. One method—not a method I recommend, but one that comes spontaneously to many—would be to beat myself up, ruminating over what a terrible person I was until my self-esteem shrank so small that it would be a wonder I ever thought I had anything to be proud of.

There is a better method, though it might seem counterintuitive. The problem with spiritual pride is that it takes something good and twists it into something bad. If there wasn't something worthwhile at the bottom of it, there would be nothing to be proud of. Pride in the ethical discipline of keeping vows was my particular poison, but pride could distort and debase any aspect of spiritual life. You could study the texts—even texts that teach humility—motivated by scholarly vanity. You could approach meditation like an athlete collecting trophies. You could revel in insights and epiphanies, lingering a little too long in the light of wisdom until it dimmed shyly, embarrassed to keep your company. Anything that was good could turn bad if it became a hook for pride. That didn't mean you should give up on trying to be good.

Is it possible to find virtue in yourself, to recognize genuine accomplishments, to honor them as worthy—and then just let them be, without letting pride put its sticky fingerprints all over them? Surely I had good models. The careful humility of each of the monks I had spent time with was a clear lesson. There may have been an odd irony in Sasaki's self-effacing reluctance to teach formally, but it wasn't humble bragging.

Had I been proud that day when he pushed me to teach? Not so much. I was too nervous to be proud, anxious at the very idea of teaching in front of someone so senior to me, and utterly focused on doing justice to the task at hand. I knew instinctively in that moment that the best I could do would be to serve as a conduit of something purer than I could ever produce by myself. It wasn't about me. Afterwards, in the surprise of having pleased Sasaki, I had felt a moment of pleasure that certainly edged on pride. And I had let it go: I was pleased that he was pleased, and we were both pleased that the Dharma had been served appropriately. That much was worth a cookie.

•

A month or so later, on New Year's Eve we did a late-night prayer ceremony marking the turn of the year. I was tired and fell asleep quickly when we finished prayers shortly after midnight. I woke up about two hours later, restless, and noticed a dim light under the door to Sasaki's room on the far side of the courtyard. Was he still up? I crossed the courtyard, and as I did, sounds from behind the door grew louder. He was reciting something. I couldn't make out the words, but his voice was intense with emotion, rising and falling dramatically. I didn't want to disturb him by knocking, so I just opened the door a crack to look in.

I drew back immediately, stunned. The whole room was flooded with a blinding light. I looked again. I could see the shrine at the wall to my left in flames. Sasaki, who sat almost directly in front of me facing the shrine, was lit by the firelight and yet at the same time silhouetted, his profile stark against a blazing circle of light, edged in tongues of flame.

What am I seeing? In a blink, a third look, and it was gone. Sasaki was sitting there chanting in the dimly lit room, just as I had seen him countless times before. Normal, except for the intensity of his voice. He didn't seem to register my presence or the open door. I shut it silently, and padded back across the courtyard. Sleep was not going to return easily that night.

We gathered as usual for prayers in the main temple early in the morning. I had decided to say nothing. I felt I had accidentally witnessed something deeply private and it was not my place to ask questions. But then Sasaki walked over to where I was sitting. He smiled and said softly, "What you saw last night was for you only." So he had been aware of my intrusion after all. It was an instruction too, in the gentlest way, that what I had seen was not to be spoken of.

But what exactly had I seen?

Is it possible to contain that blaze in reason's straitjacket? In the encounter between Buddhism and the modern world we have been quick to discard what seems alien and fanciful, and to highlight what conforms to the Western scientific worldview. When neuroscience affirms the health benefits of Buddhist meditation, we take that as a meaningful validation; the rigorous logic of the Nalanda philosophers seems proof that they share the same reasonable outlook we do. Meanwhile, we tiptoe with eyes closed around claims that push against the unexamined boundaries of our metaphysical assumptions. If we look at all, we dismiss the supernatural as superstition, the sign of a debased form of "village" Buddhism. If it doesn't match our assumptions, it can't be genuine.

In all this cherry-picking we are filtering out something important. It's not that science is wrong-headed, or that we should bend the laws of physics to accommodate the paranormal, but there is more than fits in that box. There are other ways of knowing and engaging with the world that are also valid.

Deep in the heart of Buddhist philosophy, at its most rational, is the premise that the reality we encounter in our day-to-day lives is less solid than it appears, and that it is constructed with our participation. Science doesn't disagree. From the ambiguities of quantum physics to the biological mechanisms of perception and embodied experience, our deepest understanding of how the world works is a lot less rigid and a lot more participatory than what hard-nosed common sense offers on the surface. And if it's less rigid and more participatory, then it may also be malleable in ways that surprise us.

Consider the seventh-century philosopher Chandrakirti, whose commentaries still serve as a classic textbook on that less-than-solid ontology. He was a brilliant logician who could take down his opponents' views with one hand tied behind his back, arguing entirely from their own premises, to prove that nothing exists inherently or independently of its relationships to all other nonexistent things. And yet the world is not nothing, he insisted. However much we are engaged in its construction, it's not just a product of our imagination.

Chandrakirti was also the abbot of Nalanda, which meant he had administrative responsibilities as well as academic and spiritual ones. So, when a rainstorm caused the monastery's herd of cows to shelter in a forest at an inconvenient distance and milk was needed, Chandrakirti solved the problem by milking a cow that was painted on the wall. In the telling of the story that has come down to us, there is no suggestion that this is a miracle that stakes a claim to divinity; these are no fishes and loaves. Instead there is a tone of gentle irony: A great teacher's deep knowledge of the fluid nature of reality finds a surprising, practical expression. A portal to the irrational opens right in the heart of reason. Because he was also a Bodhisattva, as well as abbot and scholar, he was concerned not only to feed those in his charge, but to shake up his students and remind them that whatever view they believed was essentially groundless, useless to cling to.

When Buddhist texts talk about *siddhis*—paranormal faculties that are said to be within reach of the most advanced meditators—they make it very clear that *siddhis* are nothing to get excited about. Clairvoyance, walking through walls, being in two places at once—such "attainments" may surface, it's said, as side effects of practice. But it would be a serious mistake to cultivate such by-products deliberately. Doing so would distract you from more worthwhile work and send you off on a dangerous detour.

And if you did happen to find yourself in possession of strange powers, it would be an even more serious mistake to advertise that fact. Worst of all—a heinous offense that would get you expelled for life from the monastic community— would be to make false claims that you had such powers when in fact you didn't. The particular peril that looms in the vicinity of supernatural powers, whether real or falsely claimed, is spiritual pride.

In the weeks that followed, I asked Sasaki for guidance on reciting the sutra. He gave me tips on pronunciation and pacing with the *moktak,* the carved wooden fish with its eyes always open, reminding us to stay alert. But beyond the technicalities, in essence what Sasaki told me was this: "When you recite, you are not reciting a text, you are creating what the words describe. Make the whole thing come alive. Witness it." A director might say those same words to an actor without calling upon supramundane powers. Was what I glimpsed through the crack of the door that night merely some further degree of impassioned imagination, an extreme form of art? Or was it perhaps a lesson from Sasaki, a jujitsu move intended to knock me off-balance? That self-discipline I had been so proud of was barely a mote of dust in the blazing vision of infinite possibilities.

The truth is, I will never know what Sasaki did that night. I don't know what "really" happened any more than I know how Fujii Guruji appeared in my dreams or how the Bengali swami came dancing with me. And that's okay. We would do well to practice knowing nothing for sure, learning to rest calmly in a place of uncertainty without casting about anxiously for answers. The things we think we know most certainly, those solid realities we cling to and never doubt, are the source of most of our problems.

In any case, what I had witnessed was not to be spoken of. That would be tempting spiritual pride. As I said, Sasaki worked hard at not having followers, and it's only now, years after his passing in 2003 when Sarnath was left feeling strangely deserted, that it seems safe to tell what I saw.

CHAPTER 10

Discipline and Discipleship

·
·
·

There are only three ways to teach a child. The
first is by example, the second is by example, the
third is by example.

—ALBERT SCHWEITZER

What brought me to Sarnath in the first place that year started
with a nudge from R. S. Sharma. When I arrived in India for
my year "abroad," Mamu-nana had recently given the convo-
cation address at the Central Institute of Higher Tibetan Studies in Sarnath. He held a very high opinion of the institute's
director and encouraged me to seek him out. As it happened,
the Venerable Samdhong Rinpoche was visiting Delhi just
then.

Elegant. My first impression on meeting Samdhong
Rinpoche might seem odd for a monk, but it has held up over
the years. I mean it not just in the sartorial sense, though he
makes the simplest robes look smarter than a Savile Row suit.
Samdhong Rinpoche is elegant in the way that a philosophical
argument or a mathematical theorem can be elegant—pared
down, effective, surprisingly original—with an integrity so

finely honed it seems an aesthetic as well as a moral choice. He wears his authority with composure and grace, and at the same time with a disarming warmth and modesty. And he speaks a perfect classical Hindi that puts most Indians to shame. "Come to Sarnath," he said. "Come to the institute." Everything flowed from that.

Though he was a monk first and had long served as an educator, both in the Tibetan schools in India and at the institute, Samdhong Rinpoche was also a cabinet member in His Holiness the Dalai Lama's government-in-exile. He was instrumental in the process of recasting Tibet's ancient political structure into a modern, democratic system of governance for the refugee communities scattered around the world, and ideally for a future Tibet. The year after we met, open elections were held for the first time for the position of Kalon Tripa, the prime minister of the government-in-exile. He ran reluctantly but won by an enthusiastic majority. He led for two terms with such skill that there was a clamor to change the new constitution so that he could run for a third term. "You're being ridiculous!" was his final response to his supporters. Retirement meant serving as the Dalai Lama's personal envoy. I admired how he could hold the spotlight with authority in one moment, and then recede into the shadows the instant His Holiness appeared. He stubbornly avoided the fanfare and elaborate protocol that Tibetans typically lay on those they deem worthy of respect, even at risk of causing offense.

When I first met Rinpoche-ji, as I came to call him, all of this—Tibet, its diaspora and politics, and the unique flowering of Buddhism in that culture—was terra incognita to me. I knew the Tibetans had come to India as refugees, but we had refugees aplenty from Bangladesh, Afghanistan, Myanmar, you name it, crowded into their own corners of every Indian city. After I ran away and the family was suddenly paying attention to Buddhism, the story came out that my Nana, the legendary Basawon Sinha, planned the route for the Dalai Lama's escape from Tibet through Assam in 1959, enlisting his connections in the labor movement there. Or at least that's what his wife Kamala told me, who was a politician herself and Minister of State for External Affairs. She remembered how they went to greet India's esteemed new guest when he arrived at Patna station on his way to Mussoorie from Assam. Basawon Sinha was the leader of the opposition party at the time and was the one, so Nani said, who convinced Nehru that Mao was not to be trusted in the matter of Tibet, and that welcoming the refugees would be consistent with India's tradition of offering asylum to troubled neighbors. But the stories didn't really stand out in my mind from much other government gossip that my family talked about. They had met Fujii Guruji too, she said, and that seemed much more interesting to me at the time. I had no idea then that the Dalai Lama was any more significant than countless other religious leaders who called India home, and certainly no inkling that he would come to be important in my own life. The only time I had set foot in a Tibetan Buddhist temple, when I was exploring in Pokhara, it seemed an alien and incomprehensible world full of angry monsters with fangs bared and eyes bulging under flaming brows. What did these fearsome images have to do with Buddhism?

At the university in Sarnath, a door opened into this world, which turned out to be not so strange after all. I made friends with young monks from Tibet, from Nepal, from regions of India like Ladakh and Kinnaur that share Tibet's culture, from different schools and lineages whose home monasteries were scattered far across the Himalayas and who had come together under one roof through the unique circumstances of the Tibetan diaspora. Before the Chinese occupation, monks from the Indian Himalayas had traveled to the great monasteries in Tibet for their higher studies, but that avenue was now closed. One of the reasons that the institute was founded in Sarnath was to accommodate these students. The culture of communal monastic life that they came from was new to me. It held a camaraderie and warmth that had often been absent from my own life. I learned it was possible to have fun in simple ways—hanging out, talking about movies and motorbikes—without feeling that I had turned my back on what mattered. These were friends who shared my vision of what mattered, who studied hard and were sincerely committed to their practice.

Because I had no obligation to follow the university's standard curriculum, Samdhong Rinpoche took me in hand and set up an ideal program. He assigned me a teacher to begin learning Tibetan language. I already had some knowledge of Sanskrit, so he threw me into the deep end with the classical texts of Buddhist philosophy and logic, and I studied Hindu schools of philosophy for comparison. I found that swimming in these waters came naturally to me. The texts opened up with an ease that felt almost a familiarity.

This feast for the intellect was served up in a style that had been customary for centuries, and probably since the time these texts were first written. Instead of the large lectures and formal classes that are normal at a modern university, I sat with my teachers one-on-one, or at most with a couple of other students, reading the text as the teacher offered commentary and answered questions. The method demanded an intense focus, a total presence, listening with one's whole self. Taking notes would have been a distraction, if not rude. You listened and you remembered. There was no fixed syllabus, no set amount of material to cover in a certain period of time. A text would take however long it took. A door seemed to open into another time, where monks had pored over these very same words. They had swum in the disorienting depths of these same ideas in just this way: side by side with an elder who was eager for them to experience an opening of the mind, a crack where the light could enter.

At first the elderly Sanskrit pandits were surprised that a young Indian was eager to study with them—even more so a young Indian of a certain class, who would be expected to aim for a career in technology or finance or some other lever of power in the modern world. Sanskrit had fallen out of fashion and they weren't expecting a revival. But then this small world pulled its strings tight. It turned out that my relatives had been schoolmates of these same scholars once upon a time, and fond memories lit up for them, as they did for me of summer vacations spent learning Sanskrit poetry with my elders. A very warm and respectful old-world congeniality prevailed, which made studying even more of a pleasure, and they clearly took joy in teaching.

Of all these encounters I took the most delight by far in my regular meetings with Rinpoche-ji. Unlike the other tutorials he set up for me, we had no set agenda and our conversation roamed freely across philosophy, Dharma, and whatever concerns life had stirred up. Our starting point was usually questions that were sparked by the texts I had been studying, and in particular those of the great Buddhist philosophers of the Madhyamaka—the Middle Way—that flourished at Nalanda, and had a special link with the institute at Sarnath.

When Buddhism was wiped out in India as successive waves of Turkic invaders repeatedly attacked the great monastic universities, and Nalanda was finally destroyed by Bakhtiyar Khilji in 1193, it was said that the books from its legendary, nine-story-high library fueled the cooking fires that fed his army for half a year. A vast body of literature was lost forever. All that survived was what had been carried by traveling monks to other lands or was already translated into other languages where Buddhism had spread. Tibet in particular was a storehouse of Buddhist texts. For centuries, Tibet's kings had sent scholars to India and hosted Indian scholars in return, who translated Buddhist literature from Sanskrit into Tibetan with a systematic precision and standardization of terms that was unprecedented in the history of scholarship. China's occupation of Tibet and the destruction of the monasteries during the Cultural Revolution once again threatened the survival of that treasure. Part of the mission that inspired Prime Minister Nehru and the Dalai Lama to found the Central Institute of Higher Tibetan Studies in 1967 was to re-translate back into Sanskrit as well as into modern languages the lost texts that had survived only in Tibetan versions. As a result, the institute attracted a very particular expertise. In its way, it was a portal to Nalanda, a conduit back through centuries to the world where these texts had originally been composed and studied.

As a child, I had seen the ruins of Nalanda when Okonogi had brought me along with some Japanese visitors for a day trip. The grandeur of what remains, however fragmented and lonely, made an impression. In those days nothing was fenced off, and I clambered up the stairs of the towering main temple for a bird's-eye view. At that height, Rajgir was just over the horizon, a day's journey for a monk walking at a deliberate and mindful pace. Below me, more than thirty acres of the campus of the ancient university had been excavated—the many monasteries that housed the student body, the lecture halls, temples, and stupas. Much more stretched beyond those stubs of brick walls exposed to the sun, acres still blanketed with farmers' fields and villages going about their business on top of what had once been for most of a millennium an extraordinary center of learning.

I've returned to Nalanda many times since then, with a gradually deepening appreciation of what this place meant, and a growing sense of familiarity. I've closed my eyes and listened to echoes of another life, the splashing of water at the well, footsteps, laughter, the drone of recitation coming from one quarter, the clap that punctuates a point of debate. But the true legacy of Nalanda, the treasure that draws me back and seduces me into conjuring memories of a fellowship among these bricks and stones, is preserved not in the ruins but in the words of the great masters who lived and taught here.

It was Samdhong Rinpoche who first opened a door in my mind and invited Nagarjuna in. He did it without ever using his vast erudition to impress, without academic jargon or a snow pile of quotations and references. He was blunt and to the point. Where other scholars seemed too often like archaeologists on rewind, brushing layers of dust on top of ideas, Rinpoche-ji lit a fuse that ran straight to Nagarjuna's dynamite. The gratitude I feel for that explosive induction is boundless.

Nagarjuna was probably at Nalanda sometime in the second century A.D., though even that minimal shred of information about his life is far from certain. Tradition pictures him circled by a halo of water serpents, the nagas who guarded the Buddha's teachings on the *Prajnaparamita*—the Perfection of Wisdom—at the bottom of a lake until Nagarjuna could bring them up from the depths. The submerged mystery of the wisdom sutras, and the apocryphal status of so many texts that may or may not be his work, belies the hard brilliance of what we know for sure that he did write, and the force of his influence on everything that came after.

It's all very well to wave a hand and dismiss this world as illusion, but what does that mean? What is real if not what lies at hand? Nagarjuna attacked the problem with logic. Rationally, rigorously, relentlessly, and sometimes playfully too, he deconstructed the concepts we take for granted. He drilled down until any attempt to place reality—things, persons, ideas, identities—in a definable box revealed itself to be absurd, self-contradictory, or incoherent at the end of the road. In the process, he knocked down every competing philosophical system of the time, but instead of offering a superior view to replace them, he pulled the rug out radically from any possible position.

He demonstrated that nothing at all exists separately and independently. Nothing is possessed of an inherent reality. The object in my hand may be a drinking glass, or a flower vase, or a pencil holder depending on how I ascribe its function, and its fragile physical nature is every bit as changeable as those labels. That same object would have a very different meaning if it were a gift from a dear friend, or an antique that's been in the family for generations, or something I picked up yesterday at a garage sale—a meaning that will become all too clear when its fragility prevails and I feel its loss.

And yet, though the object has no inherent nature, I haven't imagined it into being. This world remains very real. Causes have effects. Our actions have consequences. The only way this is possible, the only way that things, persons, concepts, and identities exist at all is as contingent lean-tos, temporary snapshots in an unceasing flux, as relational points on a map that has no hard underlying geography. The term he used to describe this interdependent reality is "empty"—empty of fundamental, inherent identity. That doesn't mean it's nonexistent. It's not a metaphysical void, but it's defined by virtue of convention and the concepts we designate as relevant.

Whatever ultimate reality stands outside this house of cards, its foundation and its sky, is entirely unknowable, because our knowing—our language, our concepts, our perception—can only touch what is, like itself, contingent, changeable, impermanent, and transitory. And even this rule, inviolable and without exception, that everything at all that exists in conceptual reality is "empty" is just one more concept and is itself empty.

Why does any of this matter? How is it more than an academic game? Because our natural impulse to see things not in all their fluid, temporary, relational contingency but as if they were inherently existing entities, separate and fixed, is exactly the same grasping at identity that is the root of all our suffering. If we can see through this illusion, we can let go of that grasp.

In some ways Nagarjuna was the perfect antidote to my questioning nature. Nagarjuna took questions, all right, but then he shredded them. You had to keep coming back with better questions. And then he showed you how ridiculous those questions were too. Instead of saying, "Don't ask questions," he would say, "No, the answer is not where you're looking, that's a dead end. Look further, deeper. Refine your question." The practice was the refinement of the questioning.

I kept coming back to Nagarjuna in part because I had been studying physics with a deep fascination since high school. I was worried too about what I would face after graduating. Perhaps a career path in science would be cover enough to satisfy my parents while I tunneled down this philosophical rabbit hole. Like many others, I was excited by the way that Nagarjuna seemed to foretell the mysteries of quantum physics with all this relational contingency and mutual dependence, his statements that were contradictory and yet true.

Rinpoche-ji was skeptical that there was much to be accomplished with that line of thinking. Scientists would happily appropriate ideas from Buddhism as long as their own worldview wasn't challenged. Nor did he see science more generally as a solution to the world's problems. It wasn't for lack of exposure or understanding. He was a regular guest at the private meetings where prominent scientists explained their work to the Dalai Lama and discussed how Buddhism and science might be relevant to each other. He didn't question the validity of scientific knowledge, but he was profoundly skeptical about the value of technology to human flourishing. Those were two different tracks, he believed, and they didn't necessarily converge.

His views had crystalized out of a deep study of Gandhi's ideas, and reached far beyond his unshakeable commitment to a nonviolent path toward self-rule for Tibet. He believed that the solution to the economic imperialism of globalization and the challenge of environmental sustainability was a return to a purely local self-sufficiency. He was worried for the Tibetan farming communities in India, where technology has been used as a rationale to monopolize access to seed. Just as Gandhi's challenge to Britain's textile industry was homespun cotton, Samdhong Rinpoche was preaching small-scale organic farming as the answer to Monsanto.

I had doubts that a retreat from technology into a simpler life could ever be a viable solution on a global scale. It was not unusual that we had differences of opinion. As often as we came to different conclusions I always felt that his starting observations were accurate and insightful. We did agree that unless ethics was part of a scientific education, then science was likely to do more harm than good.

In any case, I owe it to Samdhong Rinpoche's influence that I abandoned the idea of a career in science, though he also steered me away from a formal monastic education. In my enthusiasm for what I was learning at the institute, I was seriously considering the possibility of diving even deeper into the writings of the Buddhist masters and their Indian and Tibetan commentators. Notwithstanding the luxury of my tutorials with the pandits, the institute at Sarnath was cast in the mold of a modern Indian university. I had learned of an alternative that seemed like it might offer an even more authentic monastic education. The steady flow of refugees from Tibet and the destruction of Drepung Loseling, Sera, and Ganden—the great monasteries that had been continuously living centers of education since the fifteenth century—had led to groups of monks rebuilding those institutions from the ground up in south India. Their early years in the 1970s had been a time of hard labor, clearing the jungle plots that the Indian government had granted them, learning to farm in an unfamiliar climate, and surviving the disease and hunger that came with such bare subsistence living. By now they were well established and it was possible to study, to immerse oneself entirely in the traditional methods of a Tibetan monastic education leading to a *geshe* degree, which involved a tremendous amount of memorization as well as formal dialectical debate. It could take at least twelve years if not forty, but I saw that as more an attraction than a problem. My biggest problem at Le Moyne was that I was on track to finish far too quickly.

So I asked Rinpoche-ji very sincerely if he thought it would be a good idea for me to enter a monastery in the south to continue my studies. He answered, without any effort to be diplomatic about it, that if I wanted to become a *karmakandi*—a specialist in rituals—I should head south. The word he used implied a shrunken scope of aspiration, even if it wasn't exactly derogatory. "But you were a Brahmin to begin with," he teased. As if a preoccupation with ritual was pretty much the same wherever. "If you really want to study Buddhist philosophy, stay here with me."

It hit me: He himself had been trained entirely within that monastic system and was one of its most stellar alumni. He had worked tirelessly to keep Tibetan cultural identity and language alive in the face of very real threats of forced erasure in its homeland and slow dissolution in diaspora. And yet he was entirely willing to question the efficacy and relevance of the education that lay at the very core of that culture. I came to understand that he is a uniquely original thinker in the world of Tibetan Buddhism, immersed in the tradition and one of its most knowledgeable scholars, but also standing outside of it, with a clear-eyed view of its limitations and a willingness to shed any portion that has outlived its purpose.

His openness, his iconoclasm, and much of his thinking about education were influenced by his friendship with Jiddu Krishnamurti, and that influence was mutual. Though Krishnamurti stood adamantly outside of any religious tradition, he was a ready if uncompromising teacher and receptive to a kindred spirit. From the time of their first meeting in 1971 until Krishnamurti's death in 1986, they were frequent partners in conversation, and "K" came up often in our talks.

From my seat on the couch in Rinpoche-ji's office, or on our long walks together around the campus, I often felt like I had an ear to the door, listening in on echoes of those exchanges. It was both thrilling and humbling to realize that even as a student I was invited to participate in a similar genre of open-ended, informal, but entirely serious exploration with a brilliant scholar and practitioner. As a method of teaching, it inspired one to rise to the occasion and give one's all, transparently and without reservation, to the topic in question. And each time I came away from our conversations with a lasting sense of warmth and welcome, as much as intellectual stimulation.

Beyond Rinpoche-ji's advice against my pursuing a more formal monastic education or a degree in physics, we talked a lot about education more generally. He did encourage me to persist on an academic track, in spite of my doubts. I was disillusioned with formal education, notwithstanding the good fit I had found at Le Moyne and in Sarnath. My deliberate failing of the board exams in high school in Delhi was more than just a strategy to subvert my parents' plans. At some deeper level it was also a determination to resist an education that served no purpose other than pushing markers forward on a track toward income and respectability. Rinpoche-ji understood my reservations. In his work with the Tibetan schools and the university, he had tried to design an educational system that was not just about employment—critical as that was to the refugee communities—but focused on character development and human values. He inspired me to think carefully about an ethical education.

I had long given thought to the ethics of the Vinaya—my conversation with Sasaki about spiritual pride happened around this same time. The problems of corruption and the toxicity of power, whether in religion, politics, or business, were a frequent topic of discussion at home for as long as I can remember. As children, my sisters and I had eyed with envy the spectacularly expensive toys that were given to our playmates on festival days. Like us, their fathers were government officials. How come we didn't get any? My father sat us down and explained why he rejected the lavish gifts that others received, explained this blight of corruption that others blindly accepted. We should be proud instead of being jealous, my mother said. And we were. Better than fancy toys that would soon break was having a hero for a father.

I had pondered whether this blatant, pervasive, and entirely mundane evil was built into the human condition. Was it just the way the world works, or was it fixable? What kind of intervention, what policies, would it take to reduce the misery that those in power impose on those they govern? Samdhong Rinpoche had pondered it too, as a leader of what was for all intents and purposes a small displaced nation sheltering inside the Indian polity, obliged to negotiate its corruption as well as, hopefully, positioned to learn from the humanitarian ideals of its secular democracy. The fact that he had reflected on this as a monk, one who was highly regarded for the rigor of his own ethical discipline, inspired me, as did the clarity and maturity that he brought to bear in thinking about secular institutions from a Buddhist viewpoint.

We talked about how ethics could be taught, and what its rightful place in education might be. Should there be a formal code of conduct, something like a modern, streamlined version of the Vinaya for laypeople, that would articulate the unspoken norms of civility? Too often people adhere to a formal code of conduct only out of fear of punishment. What would it take to inspire a joyful adherence, where stick and carrot became irrelevant, where the egotistical pleasure of being seen to be good was eclipsed by the greater joy of doing good? Could one experience a self-driven motivation toward ethical behavior, like a student who is motivated to learn not by grades but by the joy of learning itself?

Perhaps adherence, no matter how joyful, to an external code of conduct, whether formally constructed or embedded in social norms, was an insufficient framework. What if the self-driven motivation that we were hoping to define was actually a form of self-regulation, just as all living organisms self-regulate? What would it mean for humans as a species, not to mention our impact on the rest of the world, if we understood ethics as the homeostatic balance of a healthy human mind, and learned to self-regulate the fear and greed that counter our deeper impulses to compassion and care?

Offering courses on ethics was not the answer, Rinpoche-ji believed. Defining a curriculum that treated ethics as a subject for study, whether traditionally as a domain of philosophy or in some more creative way, was too limited, too narrowly conceived. Instead, ethics should permeate all aspects of education. It had to be seamlessly integrated with sciences, history, literature, and every other aspect of the day-to-day conduct of scholastic life. The need for this was urgent, he insisted.

Those conversations planted seeds that continued growing in my own mind. Several years later, I was a visiting scholar at Massachusetts Institute of Technology, where I had first served as Buddhist chaplain to the institute. In 2007, I began collaborating with professors there, exploring how experiential training in ethics might be integrated into their courses. The disastrous ethical failure that manifested as the financial crisis in 2008 made the need all the more apparent. Talking to friends from high school and college who were working on Wall Street and in other financial institutions, it was clear how that hothouse environment had not only allowed but encouraged the personal greed, short-term gamesmanship, and opportunism-run-amok that then managed to latch on to every available lever of systemic weakness, the more obscure and layered in complexity the better. The players were disproportionately Ivy League graduates, or otherwise alumni of the most elite educational system that money and smarts could gain entry to. What had gone wrong? What was missing in a supposedly excellent education that had left them so ethically ungrounded? The urgency was burning.

Conditions aligned. At MIT I was in a place that was unusually open to innovation, and where the student body was moving at high speed through a pipeline to positions of influence and power in fields that would define our future. I began to reach out to colleagues, to start conversations and gather resources. What would it take to get ethics into the curriculum at the business school—not just as an abstract concept but an experiential training? How could ethics be integrated as part of best practices in engineering and in all of the disciplines where MIT so famously excelled?

Those questions, and their refinement into ever more precisely targeted questions, would evolve into the Dalai Lama Center for Ethics and Transformative Values at MIT. I'm proud that Samdhong Rinpoche supported it eagerly, and I'm grateful to him for planting seeds of inspiration.

•

Back in Sarnath, it was inevitable that our conversations turned to what it meant to be a teacher and a student together on the spiritual path. After all, there we were, like a couple of elephants in the room discussing education in broad strokes, when the most vital learning I could imagine was happening in the present moment of our exchange.

Recently, during a Q and A session after a public talk in the United States, an audience member asked Samdhong Rinpoche what it feels like to be friends with His Holiness the Dalai Lama. The question might seem trivial, but his answer, given with the careful precision that marks his every word, shone a light on the multifaceted gem that we call *kalyanamitra*—"the virtuous friend."

I was struck, first, by how very different his response was from what I've heard when Westerners who have a genuine personal relationship with His Holiness are asked that same question. They answer, however respectfully, by centering their own experience, the ego glowing in a borrowed light. After all, wasn't that the question—what does it feel like?

Rinpoche-ji didn't go there. Instead he began by noting certain aspects of their relationship that are formally defined by tradition. The Dalai Lama was his teacher, who had ordained him as a monk and conferred on him the ritual initiations that empower a student to engage in certain practices. These roles carry a weight of commitment that stretches beyond this lifetime. They preclude the equality that friends normally would expect of each other. At the same time, this particular teacher and student have also had a long collegial relationship, working together for half a century as leaders of the Tibetan diaspora and its government-in-exile. In that context, yes, he would call His Holiness a friend in the sense that we usually understand that word. He describes His Holiness with obvious delight, as easy to work with, open-minded, and flexible, and democratic in his respect for others' ideas and opinions.

But the crux of their personal history is the special notion of spiritual friendship that is embedded in the teacher-student relationship he described first. The Sanskrit *kalyanamitra* translates as "beautiful, blessed, or virtuous friend." It's the friend whose influence moves you to be a better person, the friend who helps to create the conditions that enable you to mature spiritually. Sometimes that's a straightforward proposition: A teacher embodies the qualities you aspire to and shines a light on the Dharma in ways that increase your understanding and help to integrate that understanding into your life. Sometimes it's less obvious. A teacher may see your potential in ways that you can't see yourself, may recognize conditions that are ripe for a change and strike a note that you didn't realize you were ready to hear.

It's not an exclusive relationship. Rinpoche-ji would have called Krishnamurti a *kalyanamitra,* as well as the Dalai Lama, and no doubt others too. His Holiness once said that at least sixteen different individuals fit in this category in his life. Thousands of his own students see him in that role. But the profoundly reverent way that Rinpoche-ji describes His Holiness the Dalai Lama as a *kalyanamitra*—that's how I like to think of my own relationship with the Venerable Samdhong Rinpoche.

The special quality that sets this friendship apart from what we normally understand as friendship is that it is not driven by emotional needs—"pure" is how it's traditionally described. Companionship, the security of belonging and connection, the validation of feeling seen and heard—all the normal expectations of friendship are irrelevant, and quite likely unmet insofar as those expectations are masks for attraction and clinging. Physical proximity might be part of how the relationship grows, but it's not necessarily so. The relationship doesn't fade with time and distance; it's not threatened by the things that challenge a conventional friendship. You don't feel impelled to call your teacher up and say, "Hey, it's been a while, I miss you. Do you want to get dinner?" It's not about face time and it's not dose dependent. A *kalyanamitra* isn't the kind of friend who's there for you when you're feeling down. There's no need for physical presence; the mere thought of that friendship is sufficient to lift you up.

Whatever the circumstances, respect never falters. A teacher may be playful with a student, may engage with humor and wit, but that doesn't mean you are buddies. There may well be times when you share your most personal concerns, but acting as your therapist is not part of a teacher's job description. There are examples of such relationships that have matured with age into an intimate melding of minds, where a student can complete a teacher's sentences, but even so, each one knows their place.

Respect doesn't mean that emotion is absent from the relationship. A *kalyanamitra* sparks love, gratitude, and devotion, but then steps out of the crosshairs. The emotion is not personal. It might look like devotion to an individual on the surface, but at the heart of the experience it's devotion to truth and love for the goals you share: enlightenment and alleviating suffering. It's gratitude for the guidance, inspiration, and encouragement. It's awe and gratitude for connecting with this extraordinary treasure that has been alive for millennia, with precious opportunities to engage and learn passed on in just this way from teacher to student. It's love untainted by attachment or grasping, which means that it comes with at least an inkling of how this love is "empty," as Nagarjuna would say. It's real progress on the path.

The term *kalyanamitra* can also refer to a relationship with a peer as well as to a teacher. The "virtuous friend" is then a comrade on the path whose influence nudges you toward spiritual growth. You are companions in *satsang*—a fellowship seeking truth. Truth, however, is a slippery fish. In the Buddha's most basic formulation of ethics—those first five vows—the vow to abstain from "wrong speech" is understood to include not just lying but also factual statements that are motivated by self-interest, as well as the idle gossip and flattery that sometimes motivate a facsimile of friendship. Our task is to learn how to engage with others without adding to the casually harmful noise of wrong speech, let alone any more malicious subversion of truth.

Sometimes the truth that is the most immediately relevant and powerful prod to growth is a truth about ourselves that's hard to stomach. The way that social media has re-engineered our opportunities for emotional connection, confining us within bubbles of common interest and putting tribalism on steroids, has made it more difficult than ever to hear hard truths. Anyone who doesn't share the opinions that define our self-image is sooner or later dismissed as a bearer of fake news and unfriended. Our flaws remain invisible in our own eyes until a trusted friend holds up a mirror and reveals our blind spots. But the hand that reaches out to a friend who is caught in destructive habits needs a skillfully delicate touch, free of self-righteousness and moral superiority. If it burns like a slap it provokes resistance that only creates further harm. This truth-telling is a two-way conversation, a willingness to receive as well as give criticism. A friendship of this nature that supports mutual growth is a fabric woven from interlocking patterns of caring and patience, because growth is often a very slow process.

That virtuous friend whose influence nudges you toward your better self may well be someone who is part of your life in an entirely secular context. The labels are not essential. I wonder sometimes at the strangeness of this world where we have learned to compartmentalize so many different shades of relationship—spiritual, professional, casual, buddies, with or without benefits, and who knows what else; where we have designed all sorts of technologies to feed our needs as social creatures; and yet we still hunger for deeper connection amidst the noise, and need to pay a therapist to fulfill the function that friendship has filled in older cultures.

●

The teacher-student relationship in Buddhism is not unique, except perhaps in the understanding of emptiness that throws the distinction between the role and the individual into high relief. Devotion to one's teacher is deeply embedded in many traditional cultures, not only in a religious context, but also in music and the arts—in any sphere where learning needs a long commitment of time and practice, and where the teacher serves as a model, embodying what the student aspires to.

The forms and customs that express devotion, respect, and care in these traditions have evolved over millennia. Their complex, richly layered qualities are easily lost when the tradition is transplanted to the West. If a student parrots gestures and words of respect without sensing the deep structure they arose from originally, it's like pulling on an ill-fitting coat. It's tight in all the wrong places, and the fabric itches terribly. Discipline becomes a straitjacket that sparks rebellion. Resistance festers, and sooner or later the student walks away. We've seen how detrimental that has been to Western Buddhism. The remedy of an opposite extreme drops all protocol that seems foreign, but in the process abandons the respect and reverence that set spiritual friendship apart from emotional needs. The asymmetry (that smacks of patriarchy and rankles the Western mind) reminds us that this is not about the individual so much as it is about the larger role that the teacher embodies.

The essential piece that gets lost in translation is the experience felt in older cultures as an aesthetics of reverence. If the ideal of *kalyanamitra* is to survive and be carried forward successfully in the modern world, it will not happen by diluting and debasing the original. Instead we will have to create new forms to express reverence, love, and gratitude in ways that are true to the new culture's own aesthetic. We will have to explore and understand the deep structure of spiritual friendship rather than borrowing a script to address a guru in ways that feel alien. We will need to unlearn the binary thinking that insists a teacher who is not authoritarian must obviously be a buddy. The friendship that's called beautiful, blessed, and virtuous lives in a much more interesting landscape than either of those simplistic poles.

At one point Ananda, the Buddha's cousin and attendant, offered an exuberant appreciation of this excellent friendship, "This is half of the holy life, lord: good friendship, good companionship, good camaraderie." The Buddha corrected him, "Not so, Ananda, don't say that. Good friendship, good companionship, good camaraderie is actually the whole of the holy life." The only thing that a teacher seeks in this friendship is the student's growth and liberation through their practice. There is no other motivation.

CHAPTER 11

Radical Integrity

•

•

•

The Master doesn't talk, he acts.
When his work is done, the people say,
"Amazing; we did it, all by ourselves!"

—LAO TZU

I had shown up as usual for my Tibetan lesson and was surprised to find a crowd of monks and laypeople milling around the apartment building. The commotion seemed focused just upstairs from my tutor Tashi Samphel's place. Word was that a famous Tibetan yogi had come to Sarnath for the big puja that was happening the next day, and all his disciples in the area were gathering to pay their respects.

"We should go upstairs and see him," Tashi-la said. "You should get his blessing. He is a great meditator." I was curious. I had been urged to meet any number of Buddhist VIPs who came to Sarnath on pilgrimage. They tended to be scholars or ritual masters who held high rank within the various Tibetan Buddhist lineages. I had yet to encounter anyone resembling the legendary Tibetan meditators.

We joined the flow slowly milling up the stairs, and I gleaned a bit more information about Drubwang Konchok Norbu Rinpoche on the way up. "He's very eccentric. They say he spits on people . . . You never know what he might do. He might punch you or slap you." I wasn't worried. In my wanderings I had encountered many yogis and sadhus who talked about, or even emulated, crazy wisdom masters. Eccentricity would not scare me off.

We squeezed in with at least half a dozen other supplicants. The room was barely furnished, with a single bookshelf that had a very simple shrine arranged, and a narrow bed that also served as a meditation seat, where Drubwang Rinpoche sat facing us. He had a huge mass of gray dreadlocks piled like a turban on his head. His fingers, resting on the rough blanket on his lap, had nails that curled like horns, a few inches long. He looked straight at me with a softly pensive expression.

There was no ceremony, no one was nudging me to observe Tibetan protocol—*now is the time to offer the khata, now you do prostrations*—as I had experienced on meeting with other teachers. And yet I felt an overwhelming and spontaneous urge to honor him. So I did what felt natural to me, bowing deeply to touch his feet in the Indian way. A few words were exchanged over my head, but they flew by too quickly for me to make out what was said, or maybe it was the Ladakhi spoken by the attendants. I was oddly nervous, though I couldn't say why.

When I got up he looked straight into my eyes. I felt like I was being x-rayed, naked to the bone. He gestured for me to come closer. A hush fell over the room, as if everyone's breath stopped, not just mine. He grabbed my head with both his hands. I could feel the scratch of his nails beyond his fingers' tight grip. He brought his face up close above mine, then lowered it and rested his forehead on top of my head. The weight of his dreadlocks rested on my head. I was used to the traditional Tibetan greeting that touches forehead to forehead, but this was something else entirely.

I felt like I was dissolving. My body was trembling—no, vibrating. I could feel his breath on my face as he recited something, but the sounds didn't register as meaning. My mind was blank, completely blank for a stretch of time that I couldn't measure. Then he lifted his head and gently pushed mine back, separating us as if he had just unplugged me from an electric socket. All that was left was a sense of clarity, as if a cloudy sky had cleared to blue. There was a familiarity and a certainty too in that clarity. It was a distinct feeling that would last for several days and then gradually fade, though the taste remains in memory even now.

He said nothing, just gave me the subtlest of smiles. Somehow I left the room and made my way downstairs. The attendants and a handful of others followed me out, and we gathered outside. Nobody said a word. I wasn't the only one who seemed to be in a state of shock. Then the tension broke and we were laughing and smiling and some were saying, "Well, that was wonderful!" Others were saying, "Unbelievable!" I was trying to figure out what had just happened, wondering if anything that was said in the room might hold an explanation.

I asked one of the attendants what he thought, and he said "It's beyond me. I've never seen anything like it. Usually he gives blessings by flicking a hand or gently touches the head and blows on you. Sometimes he spits instead of blowing, that's a blessing too." He said it had lasted for maybe ten or fifteen minutes. It hadn't felt that long, but I wasn't in any state to mark time accurately. Everyone agreed that something special had happened, though no one quite knew what. In any case, it seemed worth celebrating, so I bought a round of mango Frooti juice boxes for all of us from a nearby stall.

Whatever else he'd done to me, he had certainly grabbed my attention. I wanted to learn more. Between his students and others I met in the Tibetan and Ladakhi community, there was no shortage of stories about him floating around. For all the dramatic flurry of his disregard for the normal ways of the world, every story pointed to a radical integrity that made sense of his eccentricities.

He had no interest at all in the complex hierarchies of the Tibetan religious world, though all doors were open to him. He was well known to all the prominent heads of lineages, deeply respected by all, but he seemed to have no awareness of, let alone concern for, recognition and the markers of status: who was building the bigger monastery, or traveling to teach in the West, or publishing books. These were all vagaries of samsara in his view, even if they went under the label of Dharma. He was, however, absolutely devoted to the Dalai Lama. At one time when His Holiness was teaching in Ladakh, Drubwang Rinpoche showed up in the midst of the session and started doing prostrations. Not the modestly abbreviated form that most elderly people or anyone in an overly crowded room would do. No, he did an extreme version of the full body prostrations known as "the tree falling"— *ba-boom!*—dropping hard on his knees and then throwing himself out flat on the ground. Not just the requisite three times, but over and over again. His Holiness continued teaching with Drubwang Rinpoche pounding the floor—*ba-boom! ba-boom! ba-boom!*—in a corner of the assembly. Finally, with a look of concern, as if he feared the old man might have a heart attack, the Dalai Lama stopped and said, "Rinpoche, that's enough . . . enough now!" At that Drubwang Rinpoche finally took a seat.

I was told that he was one of very few people who could come and go from His Holiness's residence at will. The security detail had a standing order not to stop or question him. Drubwang Rinpoche wasn't the type to schedule appointments. He had shown up once with a large bag of cash—accumulated donations from his own followers—and dumped it out in a pile on the table, saying to His Holiness, "You travel a lot, you do a lot of good work. You have more use for this than I do." And then he walked out, not waiting for thanks.

That untethered relationship with money was a constant worry for the students who were closest to him. One day they felt the need to finally intervene. They had been on the road earlier, with Drubwang Rinpoche in the front seat of the Jeep, his dreadlocks polishing the ceiling with every bounce, when they passed a man selling small clay statues of the Buddha on the side of the road. It was a common sight in Sarnath, where pilgrims promised a potential market. Drubwang Rinpoche insisted on stopping and inspected the statues, enthusiastically pronouncing them "Good, good, good, good." He picked one out and asked the price. The vendor quoted a thousand rupees and Drubwang Rinpoche handed him the cash without a moment's hesitation, let alone any attempt to bargain him down. The students were seething. The little statue, cast by the dozens out of the cheapest material, was worth no more than twenty rupees maximum, and even a clueless tourist would have known better. The vendor had cheated their teacher shamelessly; the shame was theirs for letting it happen.

I watched him rearrange his shrine that afternoon to make

room for the clay statue, as excited as a little kid with a wonderful new toy, though I left before the big drama unfolded and learned about it afterwards from his students. One of the senior attendants was delegated to confront him. That took serious courage. Not only was Drubwang Rinpoche wildly unpredictable, he was said to have the power to take on wrathful forms. Nobody knew exactly what kind of wrathful forms, as people around him tended to shut their eyes in terror whenever things started to get crazy. So the attendant very tentatively, with eyes cast down and bowing low, said to him, "Rinpoche, the statue that you bought today . . . the statues they were selling on the road . . . those are clay statues."

Rinpoche looked at him. "So what?"

"You know, Rinpoche, they are worth twenty rupees. You gave him a thousand rupees . . ." And then the attendant squeezed his eyes shut quickly, because Rinpoche was suddenly very much larger than life.

"And you are a monk?" he shouted. "You are a monk?" He grabbed his cloth bag and pulled out a generous fistful of cash, rupee notes of all denominations, that followers had given as offerings. "This," he shouted, waving it high, "is paper! And this"—he gestured to the statue now in a place of honor on his altar—"is Buddha! It doesn't matter if it's clay or gold, it is still Buddha, our teacher. This is who gave the Dharma, this is who will get us enlightened!" He tossed the cash in the air—"Will this get you enlightened?" It showered down like so much worthless confetti.

•

A couple of months after our encounter in Sarnath, I happened to spend some time attending teachings in Dehradun. I knew that Drubwang Rinpoche lived nearby at a small hermitage near the falls at Sahastradhara, and I wanted very much to see him again. I joined the line of Tibetans and Ladakhis waiting to see him, every one of them reciting mantras under their breath, nervous with anticipation. An attendant tried to shoo me in ahead of the others, but I kept to my place. I fully intended to stay for a while, and not just pass through quickly for a blessing like most.

When I entered the hut, he was once again sitting on a narrow bed wrapped in a blanket. There was a *thangka* painting on the wall behind him, a shelf with a couple of books and a very simple shrine. A small table held a wooden cup and a prayer wheel. That was it. But the room was somehow filled with his majestic presence. He told his attendant to shut the door and he gave me that subtle smile again. We spoke through the attendant, who translated into Hindi, as I couldn't follow his dialect.

"Why have you come?"

"I don't know."

"Good. It is good not to know. So what do you want?"

"I'd like to receive teachings."

"I don't teach."

"That's fine, can I just stay here?"

He looked around, as if measuring the space. "I don't have any room."

"I'll find a place to stay in the monastery."

"Good. Go and meditate on impermanence. If you understand that, you will understand everything."

I tried asking him how to go about it, hoping for specific instructions, but even more just hoping to continue the conversation. He answered, very gently, "You know that already. Don't ask me. Just go do it. If you have questions, come back later." I did come back, as often as I could manage it. With his blessing, his students shared with me some of the instructions he had given them, and I spent a good portion of my time in Dehradun and later practicing what they had shared. But more than anything I wanted to use my time there to just soak up his presence.

His claim that he didn't teach was more deflection than truth. He was well-known for teaching the mantra that was familiar to all Tibetans: *om mani padme hum*. His emphasis on that one formula was strategic. People tended to seek him out for reasons he didn't particularly want to encourage. Tibetans wanted him to confirm auspicious dates, heal ailments, or clear obstacles that stood in the way of success. They wanted to learn about their past lives or be reassured about future ones. Other teachers came asking for him to give the most advanced of esoteric teachings, and he deflected humbly, claimed he didn't have those skills. Foreigners came asking too, even if they weren't particularly eager to take on the prerequisite commitments. They wanted him to interpret their dreams, which had seemed so remarkable in the dark of night, but to which he would only say, "It's a good dream. But just a dream. Now go practice."

He sent them all back to the essentials. The recitation of the mantra *om mani padme hum* was the most ordinary practice, universally accessible. The phrase was visible everywhere— carved into stones, spinning on prayer wheels, fluttering on flags in the wind—and repeated by all, mumbled softly or silently rehearsed. That invocation of the Jewel-Lotus cut to the most essential core of the Buddha's teachings: a lotus flower rooted in the mud of our existence, rising out of that murky pool to unfurl its petals in unsullied perfection and reveal at its heart the jewel of the enlightened mind—the Buddha's reality, our own potential—nirvana contained within samsara, the impulse to boundless compassion indistinguishable from wisdom's emptiness. There was nothing in all of Dharma, he insisted, that was not somehow packed into those six syllables sacred to Avalokiteshvara, the Bodhisattva of compassion, and in their unpacking he was a gushing fountain, the words pouring out like spontaneous poetry in a fulgent stream that left his translator gasping for some fraction of a pause to interject.

His style of teaching was very different with those students who were seriously committed and who, in many cases, had spent years meditating in retreat. It was a conversation. Questions would generate long pauses, and then he would slowly start to talk. Sometimes I sat in the corner for long stretches of time while nothing much was said. Sometimes he would just look at you. I imagine a context that was much the same when the Buddha originally taught: a gathering of a handful of students within a culture where learning happened through observation and emulation. Teaching arose organically through conversation, rather than as sermons composed for an occasion. Students held the spoken words in memory, condensed them into verse, and wove them into lifestyles and practices. Even more essential than the words remembered, filtered, and reconstructed, was the teacher's presence.

In the Jewish tradition, it's said that the disciple must learn from the actions of the teacher, even if it means following him into the outhouse. The sage's behavior is Torah to be read. You learn by observing how a teacher relates to the world around him, even—or especially—in the most mundane details. That kind of learning might well evade being captured by language. The living exemplar embodies the lesson with more nuance, more integrity and resilience in the face of the unexpected than words can ever deliver. Somehow we have lost that learning tradition. Spontaneous teachings appear to the left and right of us in exchanges that we rarely pay full attention to, let alone preserve in a way that we can pass on to others with awareness and respect.

What I saw in Drubwang Rinpoche in his every moment of engagement was a simplicity, childlike but far from naïve, that shone with a light of conscious choice. He was functioning in this world but he was not bound by its rules or priorities. His own priorities were absolutely consistent and only seemed eccentric when viewed through the lens of worldly sensibilities. He embodied a spiritual practice that was entirely pure in its motivation. He seemed to have erased all transactional calculations from his mind, and it was only the contrast with everyone around him that made him seem odd.

So much of our spiritual life involves an estimation, however subtle or barely conscious, of what our time and effort is worth: What am I going to get out of this? It's a salesman's trick. If I meditate for twenty minutes, if I carve out time for this retreat, if I shell out for a ticket for this teaching, what is my return on investment? The absorption of meditation and mindfulness practices into the mainstream has entirely repackaged spiritual motivation in terms of this cost-benefit analysis. We now have bullet points, features, and benefits to deflect us from the path: Learn to relax, lower your blood pressure, improve your focus, increase your productivity. If we haven't yet caught the bug, employers will offer incentives. We have apps to conveniently quantify our progress, and spur us to compete. The tech industry has been the most eager to convert spiritual practice into a life hack. They are early adopters by nature; others quickly follow.

If meditation and mindfulness in the grip of late-stage capitalism have become tools to boost productivity, in the hands of psychotherapists they become tools for managing emotion. They protect and shore up a fragile ego instead of serving to shatter it purposefully. They render samsara less unpleasant rather than pointing us toward liberation. Renunciation seems irrelevant when our capacity for tolerating the world's suffering and our own is so well enhanced. The medicine that should lead to awakening is being prescribed off-label as an anesthetic.

Drubwang Rinpoche would have seen the flaws of such thinking immediately. We, on the other hand, will have to expend a lot of effort to unlearn the messages about meditation that are broadcast from all corners. If I choose to say very little about the actual practice of meditation in these pages—or more precisely, the innumerably many practices that go under the label of meditation—it is because I don't want to add more noise to this cacophony. Beyond advertising the benefits of meditation, more than enough words and trees have been spent describing specific practices in detail. What is needed more urgently is attention to the motivation, the discipline, and the sense of purpose that creates a nest for the practice and will ultimately determine its outcome.

Like every other aspect of spiritual practice, meditation ideally is exploratory and experimental. We have learned to think of discipline as just showing up, the seat planted consistently on the cushion. Not playing hooky is a childish definition of discipline. A deeper discipline consists not in hammering away at the same problem with the same tool held at the same angle, but in our ability to self-correct. When we are stuck, can we find a detour to circumvent the obstacle without running off on a tangent? When we meet with unfamiliar terrain, can we explore without losing sight of the path? When we learn something new, and realize that it contradicts what we learned earlier, can we erase and redraw the map? The ability to adjust course is fundamental to the pursuit of wisdom.

●

Drubwang Rinpoche had told me to meditate on impermanence, and his students shared with me precisely how that was expressed in the Drikung Kagyu school. Each lineage has its own style of practice, the summation of many individual masters' experiences. Each has its particular language and unique poetry that sparks a glimmer of recognition in the student and illuminates the next portion of the path. But impermanence is a universal, the very ground the path traverses. Death brings us down firmly onto that ground in a way that never fails to impress the mind.

I chose to spend a lot of time in Varanasi at the ghats on the shore of the Ganges where the cremation pyres burned day and night. The dead of all shapes and sizes—small children, young men and women in their prime, the withered elderly— all revealed the specifics of how flesh and hair and skin, fat, sinews, guts, and bone each respond to the rapid oxidation of flame, and how the body emphatically becomes less than a person, merely material, and is finally reduced to a pile of ash and a few odd bits of bone.

I watched as the full spectrum of samsara's human drama played out around the undeniable physical facts. Some family members stayed briefly, some for hours. The sound of wailing, raw with loss and pain, rose above the cracking and roar of the fire. Some wept quietly. Others watched stoically. They unpacked bundles of worry in a few telling words with heavy faces lit by the movement of the flames: about the cost of the funeral, about whatever new configuration of domestic burden or debt this death would trigger. Others were happy to see the old curmudgeon finally gone, or were calculating their inheritance before the embers had died.

It got quieter at night. Sometimes I would stay until the early hours of the morning, watching the fires slowly burning down. On some nights a few tantrics would come late to practice. Sometimes they were drunk and rowdy, yelling foul language. Sometimes they were otherwise intoxicated. Eventually they would quiet down and settle into meditation. As I watched the embers of a life glowing in the darkness, I thought about impermanence.

This body will inevitably die and decay; it's a simple fact. Attachment to something that is absolutely certain to fail us is a pretty stupid response. At the same time, this body is the instrument for our every interaction with the world, the vehicle for every human connection, every relationship in our lives. When a person dies, it's their body that shimmers in our memory and that empty shell seems to contain all other traces—the stories, the voice, the mannerisms and behavior that were uniquely theirs. Even when physicality is gone, we cling to the chimera of the body.

I could go on: The way that a body's appearance biases our interactions until death levels us all. How, even after I had offered my body in service to the Dharma when I was in Pokhara, I still instinctively clung to it, if a little bit less than I might otherwise. How we normalize the fear of death's separation and loss even as we practice to face it squarely. But then something happened that brought all this home from the realm of contemplation and made it real in the most intimate way.

My grandmother died. At the age of ninety-six, she was living in the twilight zone of Alzheimer's disease, though she somehow still knew intuitively even before I arrived that I was coming to visit, even when little else made sense to her. She chose her time too, just hours after my sister Shefali's wedding had concluded. As if she knew that a day sooner would have upset everything and forced a year's postponement of the celebrations. As if she was still taking care of all of us. I had played the role of the eldest son responsibly in every respect, navigating a path that would satisfy family and tradition as well as the very discerning and determined young lawyer who was the bride. I had spent countless sleepless nights up to my neck in arrangements for 2,500 guests, and then danced and sang and partied for three more nights. The next day I found myself standing on the shores of Mother Ganga, carrying my grandmother's body to the pyre. I watched as the flames consumed her work-hardened hands and the feet I would bow down to touch every morning that we were together. I watched as her tattoos disappeared slowly into the black char and all the toothless kisses and silly dances went up in smoke. I saw that none of what mattered—the expression of love, the affection, respect, and devotion—would burn away with this corpse. It seemed perfectly right in that moment to celebrate a death with a wedding, to honor human connection and the promise of life continuing.

·

Four years later, I crossed paths again with Drubwang Rinpoche, this time in Kathmandu. As always he sat wrapped in a blanket on a narrow bed. From the *thangka* painting behind him, Mahakala glared fiercely at me, wearing a crown of skulls and trampling a corpse, his black the blackness that sucks in all colors but also the emptiness from which they emanate. His eyes bulged in wrath, just like those images at the temple in Pokhara that had once seemed so alien and forbidding, but I knew now that this was a guardian and protector and his dance with death was nothing to fear.

Drubwang Rinpoche looked quite different from when I'd seen him last. He had cut off all his dreadlocks the year before, which caused a storm of consternation. Typically, when a yogi of his stature cuts off his hair, it's a sign that his death is imminent. The response was a concerted campaign of long-life prayers, including one composed by His Holiness the Dalai Lama, and fervent pleas for him to stay alive long enough to teach another generation of students. "I don't know what all the fuss was about my haircut," he told me. "It was just getting too heavy." I suspect the truth was that he was so thoroughly at ease with the prospect of death that lightening his physical presence in preparation was an entirely natural step. It was certainly no reason for concern. Ever unpredictable, he remained with us for another three years.

CHAPTER 12

Aspirational Lives

.
.
.

Keep some room in your heart for the
unimaginable.

—MARY OLIVER

The premise and the promise of the Buddha's teaching is that
it is possible to start with this very imperfect mind that we
have right now—which feels terribly limited in its capacity,
which is fearful, self-centered, defensive, mired in sticky habits, prone to wandering in circles, and hobbled by an unseemly
load of emotional baggage. Starting from this very unlikely
raw material we can, with practice, transform it into a mind
that has a vast capacity for compassion, unselfish love, and
the wisdom to perceive reality clearly, unclouded by the bias
of our own needs and desires. Like all things that happen by
virtue of practice, the transformation is not instantaneous. It's
a process. We learn gradually; but because we're learning to
get out of our own way and uncover a capacity that was there
to begin with, however obscured, we have tantalizing glimpses
of where we are headed. We can see glimmers of dawn long

before the sun rises. Those glimmers both encourage us and help to illuminate the path. The heart instinctively reaches out to the light that beckons.

That sense of one's mind and heart being drawn toward enlightenment, intent on reaching the light, is known in Sanskrit as *bodhicitta,* which translates literally as "enlightenment-mind." It includes both an altruistic motivation—a selfless urge to seek enlightenment for the benefit of others—and an element of spontaneity. The urge is a leap of the heart, moved by compassion that contains no trace of bias, no favoring of one's own kind, no weighing of reward or reciprocity. The leap itself is liberating: It leaves ego and the illusion of self in the dust. It knows that somehow one's own sense of freedom is inextricably tied to the liberation of others.

Some of the practices that cultivate *bodhicitta* work on erasing bias by training ourselves to feel compassion toward strangers and even enemies, those from whom we expect no reciprocity or reward—not even the reward dished out by our own self-congratulatory ego. Other practices work on deconstructing the illusions of identity that we attach to our best actions. For example, we aim to transform our flawed generosity, which lingers on the giver's superiority, the valuation of the gift, and the recipient's indebted obligation, to a generosity so perfect that it makes no distinction between giver, gift, and recipient. The different ways of training in *bodhicitta* all cultivate a motivation that is purely altruistic, that cherishes others above oneself, and thus protects all other practices from being sabotaged by self-interest.

Bodhicitta is the driving force of a Bodhisattva's way of life, and that includes both the archetypal Bodhisattvas who populate the Buddhist universe as forces of compassion and wisdom, as well as our own small, imperfect, still aspirational existence as Bodhisattvas-in-training. It is *bodhicitta* that motivates the Bodhisattva, who has the option of stepping over the threshold into the nirvana of complete enlightenment, but instead keeps coming back, lifetime after lifetime, to this messy, sad existence we call samsara, to help those still trapped in this state. Because Bodhisattvas are here voluntarily, not trapped themselves, they carry a breath of nirvana with them.

There is one very particular manifestation of *bodhicitta* that is related to this notion of the returning Bodhisattva. The Tibetan belief in reincarnation holds that when individuals die who are very accomplished spiritually, they can control the circumstances of their next rebirth. For the rest of us, our next life is determined by the cause and effect of karmic conditioning, and the only control we have is to shift that causal chain by our choices and actions while we are still alive. But these spiritual masters have developed the skill to consciously direct their transition from one life to the next. They choose to be reincarnated in a time and place that favors their ability to continue practicing the Dharma and teaching others. These reincarnated individuals are known as *tulkus*.

When such a person dies, a few years later those who were close to him will search for a successor among young children of an appropriate age. They may be guided in their search by portents and prophecies, and will test whether any memory of a young candidate's previous life can confirm their identity. Many people are familiar with His Holiness the Dalai Lama's story of being found and enthroned at the age of three, recognized as a "living Buddha." A "living Buddha" simply means a Bodhisattva who has returned to this life for the benefit of others, driven by *bodhicitta*. That belief is the foundation underlying the succession of not only the Dalai Lama but of the leadership of many different lineages of Tibetan Buddhism.

When a student who was close to the deceased teacher reconnects with their *kalyanamitra*—the beloved spiritual friend who was mourned and missed and has now come back to life as a young child—it's hard to imagine a more meaningful relationship. There are student-teacher relationships that are braided like this across many lifetimes. The teacher returns to find the student again, only now the student has matured and is the elder. The teacher is the student, until the next time around. Lifetime after lifetime, they meet again, driven by *bodhicitta,* for no other reason than to help each other grow closer to liberation.

•

The first *tulku* I ever encountered was believed to be the reincarnation of one of the historical Buddha's sixteen elder disciples. Traditionally, the Elder Bakula is pictured holding a mongoose, an animal of extraordinary agility, courage, and intelligence. A mongoose can give any snake a fight for its life and also has a natural resistance to venom. The little animal is a guardian by instinct, who takes turns as sentinel outside his burrow to warn his tribe of danger. A protector who can take on the poisons of the world without being tainted or defeated, Bakula's totem is no ordinary mongoose, but one who generously spits up precious stones. These too are no ordinary gems but rather the various mental abilities and capacities of heart that are needed to reach enlightenment.

In 1917, a son was born to Ladakh's royal family. As a young boy he was recognized as the reincarnation of the Elder Bakula, and the thirteenth Dalai Lama confirmed that he was indeed one of the former students of the Buddha himself. When I first met Kushok Bakula Rinpoche, I knew nothing about his celebrated past lives. What I did know was that this very elderly monk in Tibetan robes was a good friend of both Fujii Guruji and Sasaki. He was also India's ambassador to Mongolia, and before that had been Ladakh's representative in parliament. Which placed him, curiously, in the orbit of my own family's elders, in particular Kamala Sinha who had served both as a member of parliament and as Minister of State for External Affairs, and who introduced "Kushok-ji" to my parents.

Bakula Rinpoche was one of the people whom my parents leaned on for advice when I first set my heart on the religious life. Aside from being the only Buddhist monk they knew, he was very highly esteemed in government circles as an accomplished diplomat. He had been a guiding light in Ladakh through the upheaval and aftermath of Independence and the transition from colonial rule to democracy, and then held a very sensitive place firmly and calmly in the long-simmering tensions between India and China. He impressed Nehru both with his skills and his concern for the Ladakhi people, and he eventually held several cabinet positions as well as heading the National Commission for Minorities. In short, he was everything my family respected most. Perhaps they saw some hope that if such a statesman could also be a monk, I was not entirely lost to the world. He reassured them that he knew the Japanese monks very well and my family needn't worry. I was in good hands; it would be best to wait and see how things unfolded.

For his part, Sasaki was eager for me to meet Bakula Rinpoche, and he brought me along for a visit when his friend happened to be passing through. Bakula Rinpoche seemed frail and spoke very slowly, with a presence that was gentle and yet stern at the same time. I was around twelve then, and what struck the younger me most memorably on our first encounter was his physical appearance. His huge, triangular head atop a tiny body made him look like an alien from a science-fiction movie. We had a polite conversation where he inquired about my family and encouraged me to study hard. What I did at school could also make a contribution to Dharma, he echoed the by-now-familiar line.

When my family moved to Delhi, my parents saw him more often. When I was helping lay the groundwork for building the stupa in Delhi, I took the opportunity to call on him, as he was the chief patron supporting the project and his influence could shift obstacles. I enjoyed our visits because he offered a uniquely safe space. My parents could raise no objection to my being there, and there was a quiet Dharma connection between us. When time allowed, I would grab the chance to ask a question about the texts I was studying, and he might inquire about my plans or how I was doing personally.

In the meantime, I got brief glimpses of his work as a diplomat when more urgent calls interrupted our time. He seemed to manage it all with an air of quiet simplicity that belied the stakes in play, and with no personal agenda, unlike so many politicians I had observed. I looked up to Bakula Rinpoche, and not only with the same respect that my parents held for his political accomplishments, which were more than remarkable. It impressed me even more that he reconfigured the domain of possibility of what a monk could be.

"Rinpoche-ji, do you have time for a question?" Sometimes I ventured beyond asking about texts, hoping he would talk a little about the questions that his very existence had planted in my mind.

We had a conversation once about what sort of economic policy the Buddha might have designed if he were alive today. It would lean a little toward socialism, Bakula Rinpoche thought, structured around shared ownership and avoiding the personal accumulation of wealth. I remember asking another time how a monk's understanding of emptiness and the illusory nature of this world squared with an ambassador's engagement with that same world. His answer touched on how the conventional world continues to operate by its own rules regardless of the ultimate nature of this reality, and how compassion keeps us from falling into the nihilism that misconstrues emptiness as signifying that this world is meaningless. That first answer to a question that in one form or another has dogged my own life has held up well. In practical terms it comes down to how elaborate an illusion we are capable of diving into without losing our bearings. The labyrinths of politics or business are much more densely woven and highly wrought fantasies than the thin membrane of illusion of a contemplative life of simplicity. With the hindsight of my own experience, I can appreciate even more deeply the extraordinary skill and grounded awareness that Bakula Rinpoche brought to his work.

It was never just politics for politics' sake. He was seriously committed to his role as a peacemaker in a fraught region, and to the welfare of the Ladakhi people and of India's many marginalized groups. The beginning of his posting to Mongolia coincided with the collapse of the Soviet Union and Mongolia's democratic revolution, and he took the opportunity to support the revival of Buddhism in a country where it had been long suppressed. "Everyone is going to the West," he said. "It's easy to go to the West." Mongolia was an entirely different challenge. Bakula Rinpoche helped to rebuild temples that were destroyed in the Soviet era, and he ordained monks, made arrangements for Mongolians who wanted to study in India, and invited teachers to Mongolia. As a sign of both the affection and respect that Mongolians felt toward Bakula Rinpoche, they called him *Elchin Bagsh,* or "ambassador-teacher," blending the roles of diplomat and spiritual leader.

It was Bakula Rinpoche who also gave me my first glimpse of Rimé, though I didn't know the term for it at the time. Historically, the inclusive Rimé ideal arose in the nineteenth century in response to sectarian tensions that were dividing Tibetan Buddhism, and as a counterweight to the power of the dominant Gelug school. Given that Bakula Rinpoche was himself a Gelugpa, Tibetans don't usually identify him as Rimé, but he embodied its nonsectarian vision in a deeper way that impressed me. Even though he was a Gelugpa himself, he honored Mongolia's historical relationship with the Sakya school and was instrumental in its revival there. Bias and loyalty never built walls in his mind. His friendship with the Japanese monks and with many Theravada monks was highly unusual in the Tibetan sphere. His ecumenical spirit wasn't just a matter of institutional choices and policy; it was a genuine embrace of spiritual friends—*kalyanamitra*—across ancient divides. He was moved by the dreams that both Sasaki and Fujii Guruji had for the revival of Buddhism in India, and helped instrumentally in the building of the temple in Sarnath as well as Fujii Guruji's stupas. They in turn felt a resonance with his vision for the restoration of Buddhism in Mongolia and supported his projects there. Bakula Rinpoche's photo had a place of honor in the main shrine at the temple in Sarnath, and Ladakhi pilgrims who traveled there knew they were welcome to stay.

The combination of his diplomatic skills and inclusive Rimé spirit led Prince Philip to recruit him to the Alliance of Religions and Conservation, an ecumenical group of religious leaders creating environmental programs. At a formal dinner for the group at Buckingham Palace, Bakula Rinpoche found himself seated next to the Queen. He had to explain that as a monk he didn't eat past noon, but he was eager to honor Her Majesty's dinner invitation so he would happily accept a cup of Darjeeling tea as his meal. If that was awkward, she was nevertheless so intrigued by his conversation—his humility, his candor, and his thoughts about climate change and the world's future—that she hardly spoke with anyone else all evening, for which she apologized afterwards to the rest of the company.

The last time I saw Bakula Rinpoche was when he traveled to Tokyo to deliver a eulogy at Sasaki's memorial ceremony. When Bakula Rinpoche himself passed away not long after, he was said to remain in *tukdam,* a meditative state that continues long beyond physical death but without the body's normal decomposition. It is a sign of a most highly accomplished practitioner, and a reminder that this extraordinary diplomat was an equally extraordinary contemplative.

Bakula Rinpoche's model of open encouragement for others whose practices and traditions were quite different from his own came at a specially meaningful time in my own life. The extremity of awe that surrounded the Lotus Sutra in the Japanese schools I was immersed in often seemed implicitly to devalue the Buddha's other teachings and feed sectarian pride. I was learning to argue politely about that, and other points, with teachers that I revered, and it helped to know that one could be not only respectful but profoundly devoted to someone, and still hold a different opinion.

Historically, the Buddha himself avoided pronouncing one teaching superior to another. He recognized that people have different dispositions. There is no one practice that suits every mind perfectly, no single story that touches every heart equally. Whether it's an ancient lineage in Asia that exalts its own tradition above all others, or a modern remix that claims to have distilled the true essence of Buddhism from its cultural dross, any sense of superiority is mostly projection. The shower of Dharma is like rain that falls evenly everywhere; how and where it's absorbed depends on the nature of the soil that receives it.

·

I sometimes had the sense that Bakula Rinpoche was quietly looking out for me with his protective mongoose in the distance. He would ask how things were going with my parents, and though there wasn't much to say, I felt that he cared—it wasn't just politeness. He was the one who suggested to Sasaki that construction work on a stupa or temple—physical labor in a devotional setting—would help to balance my studious predisposition, which carried the danger of "*geshe* pride"—puffing oneself up over book learning and scholastic debates. That suggestion was passed on to the other Japanese monks and followed me to Lumbini.

And then at some point, Bakula Rinpoche mentioned to my father that he thought I might be a *tulku,* the reincarnation of a teacher from Kinnaur that he had been very close to, and that he wanted to recommend me as such to the Dalai Lama. My father dismissed the notion. Rebirth was a familiar concept in his Hindu upbringing, but he was more than a little puzzled when Bakula Rinpoche tried to explain the very alien idea of deliberately tracking down somebody's consciousness after their death. Though he respected Bakula Rinpoche too much to say so, I think he saw it as a ploy, another tactic the Buddhists had come up with in their ongoing campaign to claim his son. Bakula Rinpoche acknowledged that it might well be problematic and even possibly have political repercussions if the Tibetans started discovering *tulkus* among the children of prominent and well-connected Hindu Brahmin families. They dropped the conversation. The topic would not come up again or interfere with the long friendship my parents enjoyed with Bakula Rinpoche, and it wasn't until many years later that I even learned about it.

Although the notion of rebirth, returning lifetime after lifetime in a cycle that ends only with the liberation of enlightenment, is deeply embedded in Buddhist thinking and familiar to Indian religions more broadly, the *tulku* phenomenon of consciously directed reincarnation is unique to Tibet and the Himalayan regions that share the culture of Tibetan Buddhism, and began there only in the early thirteenth century. Bakula Rinpoche's link to one of the Buddha's first disciples is an unusual twist in the story, not at all typical of a Tibetan *tulku*'s lineage. None of the great Nalanda masters of India are on record as having their reincarnation identified. And yet the idea is consistent with much that does appear in the sutras. The Buddha often refers to past lives or predicts how a person might come back in the future, and many sutras mention Bodhisattvas who remain in the cycle of samsara out of compassion.

What sets the Tibetan custom apart is its emphasis on formal recognition, and the power and veneration that result from recognition. The recognition of *tulkus* determines succession to almost every seat of power in the Tibetan Buddhist world, and the rampant proliferation of *tulkus* in recent times has created its own class system. There are problems, both personal and societal, that result when toddlers are raised with unquestioning veneration within the bubble of an entourage, and then presented as fund-raising attractions and showered with devotees' wealth. When *tulkus* are recognized repeatedly within the same family, succession becomes a long-term business plan and a strategy for maintaining power and influence. To the system's credit, a *tulku* is expected to repeat the prescribed course of studies and spiritual training in each lifetime. Their previous accomplishments may put them on a fast track, and some indeed outshine their predecessors. The problems arise among those who rest on the laurels of past lives.

As Samdhong Rinpoche, himself a *tulku* who was discovered at the age of five, once told me, "It is an institution that in many ways has outlived its purpose." That may be true whether *tulkus* are recognized authentically by traditional methods or merely certified by the Ministry of Religion of the Communist Party of China, which now claims the authority to determine *tulkus* of its own choosing. I prefer to think of a world where countless unrecognized living Buddhas are quietly going about their work.

The danger is not only the power that inheres in the role and the corruption that naturally attaches to power, but the damage that comes of a false valuation of a teacher. It's no different from an Evangelical preacher who calls himself a prophet. Trusting a teacher as a spiritual guide should depend on deeper qualifications than a title and fame based on a predecessor's merit. The title "Rinpoche," which pops up everywhere now, was never meant to be an inherited title attached to a position. You shouldn't call a teacher "precious one" until you genuinely feel that their presence in your life is very dear and valuable. Curiously, the teacher from Kinnaur that Bakula Rinpoche mentioned to my father lived at the farthest distance from the pomp and circumstance that normally surrounds a *tulku*. He was, however, entirely immersed in a life dedicated to *bodhicitta*.

> *Like the elements of earth and space,*
> *May I be the ground that sustains*
> *The life of countless beings*
> *In their every need.*
>
> *May I be a source of life*
> *For living things of every realm*
> *To the farthest reach of space*
> *Till they escape samsara's pain.*
>
> *Like the Buddhas of the past*
> *Who gave birth to bodhicitta*
> *And honed the Bodhisattva's*
> *Way of life,*
>
> *Likewise for the sake of all*
> *I also vow to nurture bodhicitta*
> *And learn my way, step by step,*
> *Along the Bodhisattva's path.*

There are times when you are reading, and particular verses burn a hole in your mind. The words seem to point beyond themselves, as if their sound echoes down a deeper tunnel of your being. The candle in your mind that illuminates the marks on the page somehow moves closer to your heart and you feel its warmth.

At lessons in Sarnath on the great texts of Buddhist philosophy, on Nagarjuna, or on Shantideva's verses on the Bodhisattva's Way of Life, there were always layers of commentary and intertextual references from different authorities. Many were centuries old, but a few were modern, and one name that came up often—Khunu Lama—always startled me a little. When I asked more about him, a wealth of stories surfaced.

Khunu Lama was not recognized as a *tulku* himself. Nor was he ever initiated into a monastic community, in spite of the fact that he spent many years studying and teaching at several different monasteries. He was born in the late 1800s, around the same time that Fujii Guruji was born, and that Swami Vivekananda was addressing the World's Parliament of Religions in Chicago. He came from Kinnaur, in the foothills of the Indian Himalayas, from a prosperous farming and trading family who were devout Buddhists but opposed his desire to travel for study. He left home around the age of eighteen so suddenly that he didn't stop to put on his shoes, and he never really stopped traveling from that point on.

He lived an itinerant life like the forest dwellers of old, a rolling stone unencumbered by possessions, often passing for a beggar but carrying a vast treasure secretly in his mind. He roamed through much of Tibet and India, but his travels weren't random. He was constantly in search of particular teachers to study with, drawing from all the Tibetan lineages as well as many lay teachers living in obscurity. He made a point of learning the languages deeply—both Tibetan and Sanskrit—as a prerequisite to the study of the religious texts, and gained a reputation for extraordinary scholarship. His expertise in Tibetan grammar and poetics was famous, to the point of inciting dangerous jealousies among native Tibetans. The eclectic range of his studies was extremely rare given the sectarian divisions that roiled Tibet at the time. He was never affiliated with any one lineage, with any monastery or institution.

Soon after the Dalai Lama escaped to India in 1959, he made efforts to locate Khunu Lama, who was rumored to be in India at the time. It was no easy task to find someone who kept such a low profile. He shunned attention and had a habit of disappearing whenever his reputation caught up with him. When people came to pay their respects, he would have an assistant place a huge padlock on the outside of his door as a deterrent, and slide the key under the door to him. Hours later he would slide the key back out again and knock quietly to be let out.

The Dalai Lama sent emissaries to all the Buddhist pilgrimage sites, to all the places where Khunu Lama was known to have taught, and found no trace of him. Finally, he was accidentally discovered, living incognito in a Hindu Shiva temple in the middle of Varanasi. When the emissary knocked on the door of his small closet of a room and asked if he would meet with the Dalai Lama, he said no, he wasn't feeling well. His Holiness was actually waiting downstairs and would not be put off, so then Khunu Lama demurred again because he didn't have a chair to offer his guest—an old blanket was his only furnishing. But His Holiness insisted, so they met standing up in the tiny room, and the Dalai Lama asked Khunu Lama to teach the younger *tulkus* who had accompanied him into exile, and to teach him personally as well. That was how pretty much everyone who's anyone of a certain generation in the exile community, of all lineages, received teachings from Khunu Lama, and how he became a key to the preservation of many Tibetan Buddhist teachings that otherwise would have been lost after China's occupation and the destruction of the monasteries.

His students describe him as looking like a beggar, wearing a ragged woolen *chuba* too short for his tall frame, his glasses tied together with string. He avoided ritual and the trappings of practice, never owned a statue, never did a formal retreat, but he also never interrupted his practice. Those closest to him never saw him sleeping. He ate just once a day and very simply—anything more would be a waste of precious time. The Dalai Lama's sister recounted how she once asked Khunu Lama for a blessing and instead of the customary red cord that most lamas would give, he pulled a thread from his own fraying coat. He apologized that he wasn't one of those wealthy lamas who handed out fancy silk cords, but it carried his prayers and blessings nevertheless.

When the Dalai Lama asked Khunu Lama to teach him personally, one theme among others that he specially re-quested was Khunu Lama's dearest, most constant preoccupa-tion. *Bodhicitta* was the subject he taught most eagerly and on which he wrote a poem of praise every day. He embodied *bodhicitta* with all his being. It didn't matter how great a scholar he was, how his knowledge of Sanskrit could unlock nuances of Shantideva's and Nagarjuna's writing that few others could fathom, the teaching was never just theoretical. When the Dalai Lama once asked Khunu Lama to pray for the people of Tibet, Khunu Lama was reluctant. He couldn't possibly do that, he said, as it was His Holiness who was their leader and should pray for them. He could, however, pray for Mao Zedong to experience *bodhicitta* and be moved to change his policies toward Tibet.

Khunu Lama was categorically different from any teacher of his time, lay or monastic. Unfettered by any affiliation, any lineage, any institution, he was an outlier even in the context of Rimé, which advocates for a solid grounding in one's original lineage as a basis from which to explore others with an open mind. During his time in India, and particularly in Varanasi, he not only made his home in a Hindu temple but also studied with followers of Shaivite and Vedanta schools and taught them in turn about Buddhism. He was eager to learn about history, economics, literature . . . There were no boundaries around his intellectual curiosity, or in any other aspect of his life. He welcomed female students, which was rare for men of his generation, and nuns were among his most devoted disciples.

•

A few years ago, I visited the Hindu temple in Varanasi where Khunu Lama had lived. It has a curiously ecumenical history. It is said that a particular Shaivite teacher so impressed the Muslim Mughal emperor Aurangzeb that he gave the teacher money and land to build the temple. It's a very colorful place, brightly painted, but for one brief, strange moment, I saw it in black and white. Not from the angle I had where I stood in the courtyard, but from the doorway of a particular room on the second floor overlooking the courtyard. Yes, that was Khunu Lama's room, the swami who looked after the place told me.

There's a peculiar irony in the suggestion that I might be Khunu Lama's *tulku,* because it's hard to imagine any teacher in the realm of Tibetan Buddhism who was less involved than he was in the status and ceremony that surrounds a *tulku.* I don't deny that I feel an affinity toward him, and a deep connection that is a little mysterious. But given that Khunu Lama shunned the limelight and went far out of his way to avoid recognition, it would be contradictory—a betrayal of his spirit—to seek recognition in his name. The bond that I feel with him serves no purpose unless it motivates me to hold him dear as a role model. To see Khunu Lama's character as an aspirational ideal is a worthy endeavor, and I've taken it to heart. Not a single day goes by that I don't call up his image in my mind.

The fuss over *tulkus* and reincarnation turns on a particularly human fallacy of uniqueness. We all dearly want to be special, or at least perceived as special. There is a story of a rabbi praying in the synagogue who is crying loudly, "O Lord, I am nothing! I am nothing!" A second rabbi is moved by his fervor and joins him, echoing, "O Lord, I am nothing! I am nothing!" The janitor too is carried away and cries, "O Lord, I am nothing!" Upon which one rabbi whispers to the other, "Now look who thinks he's nothing!" Even as we aspire to tame ego, we are still protecting some figment of that ego. The same spiritual pride that Sasaki named rears its head again. We all secretly think that we are the chosen one. And if we aren't the chosen one, then we at least want to be part of the special inner circle that surrounds the chosen one.

The pride that lives inside the fallacy of uniqueness is tied to the notion of the "ego of institutions" that Sasaki also identified. That same sense of a superlative self feeds tribal loyalties and religious conflict, from petty sectarianism to armed crusades. The embracing spirit of Rimé that Bakula Rinpoche and Khunu Lama embodied is an obvious antidote to sectarian pride, but it has a deeper power too. In its most fully realized form, Rimé means not just an open-minded willingness to consider other views, but the absence of attachment to any view. It's not about the content of any particular view so much as it is a way of holding the container more loosely. The mind learns to stretch to embrace ideas that may seem to be contradictory, without the stress of cognitive dissonance. It's a way of living comfortably with mystery. And in that place of ease, where attachment to any position or view begins to relax, the grasp with which we cling to our self begins to relax too.

The longing to be special has a way of surviving stubbornly, returning again and again, relentlessly undead. Even the sense of a vocational calling, which should be a calling to humility, sets us apart and revives the fallacy of our uniqueness. We are not content with the proposition that we all have the potential to become Buddhas and that we will indeed become Buddhas eventually. We want to be further unique, and that desire spawns fresh narratives of grasping and attachment.

But there is another ego-shattering antidote that Khunu Lama taught by example, in the equalizing power of *bodhicitta*. When we begin to realize that everyone else is just as unique as we are, and that our own very special potential for enlightenment is inseparable from that compassionate leap of the heart that wants every other unique individual to be freed from suffering—when we can bow humbly like the Bodhisattva Fukyo to every person we meet, because they too are a special and unique Buddha in the making—then we will have gotten our sabotaging little selves out of the way. The simple truth is that we are all manifestations of our previous selves, whether we are famous *tulkus* or just the continuing flow of a more obscure karmic stream. Who we are right now is all we have to work with. But *bodhicitta* allows us to see the possibility and the hope of enormous positive transformation in all of us. There is no better remedy for the destructive clinging to uniqueness that is the tribalism plaguing our world today.

CHAPTER 13

A Spiritual Giant

.
.
.

> Silence is God's first language; everything else is
> a poor translation.
>
> —THOMAS KEATING

"Our Father who art in heaven, hallowed be thy name . . ."

The words swept with the force of a sonic boom through the full-capacity crowd that filled Room 10-250 at MIT, where the voices of so many titans of science seemed to still be echoing a moment earlier. The monk who spoke them had the look of a Jedi master, strikingly tall in the black and white of his Trappist habit and heavy leather belt. Father Thomas Keating had seemed taken aback when I came up to the podium at the end of his talk on contemplative life—which had been quite safely "spiritual" rather than religious—and asked in a whisper if he would recite the prayer. "Here? Now? Are you sure?" he whispered back, visibly surprised.

Then, after a long, settling moment of silence and a deep breath, he began. His voice carried something more than the words, something far beyond the familiar formula. I felt as if a thunderbolt had passed through my body and hit ground, and the stillness of the hall where his words hung suspended in the electrified air told me I wasn't the only one. On the final amen, it was as if we all came out of a trance. The dean came up to me afterwards and acknowledged that something special had happened in that moment: "Whether or not I agree with Christianity is a separate issue, but that was incredibly powerful!"

Thomas asked me later what had prompted my request. I had no idea. It was entirely spontaneous. I knew the prayer, of course, from countless recitations at school in India, though never spoken with the gravitas that Thomas brought to it. And I had led prayers myself at MIT in my role as the institute's first Buddhist chaplain, but never anything like this, so encrusted with the weight of Christian tradition that it seemed a transgression in this hyper-secular setting.

I call him Thomas because that was what he insisted on, in spite of the fact that it felt more than awkward to address someone I respected so deeply, who was almost sixty years my elder, with that American informality. And doubly so because he persisted in calling me "Venerable Tenzin" with a teasing, contrarian twinkle.

I had first met the Trappist monk who led a movement to revive the method he called "centering prayer," which he traced back to the desert fathers, a few years before I invited him to speak at MIT. We had shared the stage at an interreligious gathering in California, and he was assigned to introduce me. I was expecting the routine—reading off the bio text provided—as we had just met and had only a couple of very quick conversations that morning. But Thomas added his own thoughtful observations to the bio, which surprised me. He had clearly observed me carefully in our few minutes together. The humility implied by his attention impressed me when I was quite literally nobody and he was at the pinnacle of the social hierarchy that we inhabited at that meeting, let alone in the bigger picture.

We crossed paths at a few other meetings, and each time I was struck by his openness and insights into Buddhism and other faith traditions beyond his own. He seemed to speak from an insider's understanding and yet somehow avoided any hint of a usurper's appropriation. It was as if he belonged to a larger family of contemplative mysticism; he knew well the particulars that delineated these cousins from those, but the family feeling made such boundaries a cause for curiosity rather than competition or conflict.

•

That unexpected prayer at MIT somehow opened a door to a new chapter of our friendship. We decided to go together on a kind of monks' magical mystery tour, visiting universities and speaking together to promote the idea of the contemplative life to students, exploring it as a wellspring of human potential rather than a religious endeavor. It was an extraordinary experience to spend that time with Thomas.

"We had to go through all the trouble of Vatican II to reach a decision that people like Venerable Tenzin could go to heaven!"

"The Buddhists already had thirty-three heavens. We had room for everybody!"

As odd as it might seem for someone committed to exploring the depths of contemplative silence, Thomas was an extrovert who thoroughly enjoyed being on stage in front of people. His sense of humor was contagious and I couldn't help but catch it too. But it was not for show; underneath his playfulness was a prodding curiosity that could loosen old habits of thinking and spark a seriously meaningful exchange. That curiosity stretched far beyond matters of faith. He was widely read and could speak with authority on any number of subjects. He kept himself current, particularly in psychology and science.

Thomas invited me to spend some time at his monastery at Snowmass in the mountains of Colorado, where he had hosted what he called an "interspiritual" dialogue intermittently over some twenty-five years. The discussion that we began publicly gradually became a more private conversation, and after several visits we found ourselves in a place where we could listen deeply, wrapped in a beautiful fabric woven of our agreements and disagreements, our separate worldviews, and our shared silence. The opportunity to sit in comfort with this spiritual giant has been one of the most unexpected gifts of my time in the United States.

I had long been frustrated by the shallowness of so much of what passed for interfaith dialogue in American academia. An awareness of the boundaries—now real, now tenuous—between religions, and the tensions both fraught and creative in their interactions, had been woven through every aspect of my life since early childhood. My relationship with my parents had of course been one continuous interreligious debate, but even earlier I remember ignoring my grandmother's warnings not to eat at the homes of Muslim friends. My buddies and I knew when the best meals were served on one another's festival days and we filled our bellies with a happy disregard for the religious rules that sought to divide us. My commitment to Buddhism never got in the way of my love for Sufi poetry and I spent many hours in Delhi's mosques carried away by the passion of qawwali singing.

The threat of religious violence, or what in India was termed "communal" violence, was always present too. When the news of Reverend Nabatame's death reached me in Syracuse, part of my response to the shock was to seek out opportunities for dialogue with other faiths. Surely there was a way to cultivate understanding that would make violence avoidable. Le Moyne seemed fertile ground for that effort. Though it was a Jesuit college, my advisor there was a rabbi, Michael Kagan, whose guidance I welcomed during a time of confusion and culture shock, and with whom I so much enjoyed studying Hasidic literature that I even entertained the idea of entering a yeshiva.

By the time I was accepted for graduate studies at Harvard Divinity School, I had lost patience with the easy resort to repeating, "My religion is good, your religion is good." I was ready to grapple with problems that I knew were deeply entrenched, where real harm had been done. I wanted to see genuine engagement that would make a difference where it counted. So when the orientation session on my first day there offered up a mix of vague abstraction and vacuous platitudes on the subject of interreligious understanding, along with self-congratulatory gestures of inclusion, I tuned out and left my seat for a quick errand to drop off some paperwork across the way. The real interruption came moments later when I found the office deserted, the administrative staff glued to a television at the back of another room, and the country irrevocably changed.

Before the chaos of September 11th had subsided into a new normal, with Islamophobia on one side facing off against Muslim extremism on the other, I knew that there was some very hard work in front of us. It wouldn't be accomplished by preaching to a choir that was sequestered within academia or by respectfully patting one another on our multicultural backs.

In the conversations that came up during my time at Harvard, there was much that was interesting and useful, particularly from those who brought a sociopolitical viewpoint to the analysis. But there was also a reigning confusion that refused to distinguish between ethnic violence and religious violence, between the repercussions of colonialism and some supposedly inherent vein of fundamentalism in Islam. There was also a clinging to the safe zone of the ivory tower. No representative of Evangelical Christianity was ever invited to speak, let alone any Muslim extremist. Those Muslims who were welcomed were likely to be Sufis, who have never caused violence anywhere. Nor was there any outreach that would have brought our dialogue into the daylight of mainstream Christians or Muslims. A hope for a more peaceful, inclusive society was articulated, often with passion and clarity about the injustices that had led us to our current state, but never with a vision for what unique resources our spiritual practice could bring to the table or what practical tools might turn that hope into reality.

Conversations with Thomas were an entirely different matter, beginning from a radically different set of premises. We were designing the tools. So-called interreligious dialogue, he believed, served to protect institutions and dogma, and played on the surface of our external perceptions of one another. He focused instead on what he called "interspiritual" discourse, which centered on our common humanity and how we each approached contemplative practice as the wellspring of religious faith.

In this place, we start with being human. We aren't just representatives of our separate religions; we are individual human beings, with interests and goals, personal histories and relationships. We have each come by our faith in particular ways. Over time, Thomas and I shared with each other our memories of how we each found our way to the monastic life, and our parents' resistance to that irrevocable sense of calling. So much was terribly familiar. He was raised in a bubble of wealth and privilege, his father a successful lawyer who assumed that Thomas would follow in his footsteps and saw the Ivy League education he provided as having gone to waste. We agreed that, even with years of experience in teaching (though his was vastly more than mine), our families were the toughest audience we could ever remember explaining our faith to.

Buddhist, Christian, Hindu, or Muslim, there are reasons for the stories we tell ourselves about our place in the universe and what it means to be alive; there are stories behind the stories. The point of engaging in dialogue with one another's beliefs is not to undermine or invalidate them, but to bring understanding to the process of how our views are constructed—and therefore how other views, differently constructed, can be equally valid even if we don't share them. We can examine our beliefs in a way that makes space not just for agreements but also for genuine challenges. Sometimes those challenges are reconcilable, sometimes they are not. But we can reach the understanding that they are not reasons to resort to violence, or to treat someone with disrespect. Or, in the language of Rimé, we can learn to be less attached to our views. There is a multiplicity of ways to be right, and any claim that our own views are exclusively right is the same fallacy that spurs the desire to feel singled out individually as special. One way to know that we are not specially chosen is to recognize how we all equally desire to feel chosen.

The focus on our common humanity does not assume sim-plistically that all religious experience—or even all profoundly spiritual or mystical experience—is the same on the inside, merely with different labels slapped on the outside. A particu-lar joy I found in conversation with Thomas was the ability to examine our separate traditions closely through the language of practice. We could get wonkish about details—how the tra-ditional Benedictine practice of *Lectio Divina* overlaps in some respects with mantra practice; how the experience of coming face-to-face with the divine in the practice of center-ing prayer that Thomas developed has overtones of the non-dualist states described in Vedanta; how the progression of increasingly subtle states of stillness in the Buddhist practice of *shamatha* meditation maps, or doesn't, to the deepening experience of silence in centering prayer. The vast body of Buddhist literature that has evolved around its practice tradi-tions often uses a language of such encyclopedic range that much teaching inevitably happens prescriptively rather than from direct experience. So it was a delight to hear Thomas speak of the nuances of different shades of silence and stillness with a fresh precision and immediacy of expression that comes only with first-hand personal experience.

"God's first language is silence," he used to say. "The rest is all bad translation." Over the years, the ins and outs of in-terspiritual dialogue faded from concern and became a mem-ory. We talked less and spent more time in silence together.

•

"Tenzin, I'm dying." His big smile seemed incongruous, but there was no question that it was genuine.

"It doesn't matter, I'll find you in a couple of years. You'll reincarnate, whether you like it or not."

We joked in the face of death, but its looming presence was very real. Ten years ago Thomas's health began to fail and he cut down on his travel. Then he bounced back a bit, but over the last several years, each time I saw him I thought it would be the last.

"Tenzin, I'm dying."

"I've heard that before. I just don't believe you anymore."

"No, no, no. It's wonderful!"

Each time I came to visit, death was the first topic of conversation, and each time he was a little more joyful, a little more radiant, glowing with peace. He was waiting to die, but the waiting held no anxiety, no fear, no concern for when it would happen, not even the anticipation of something glorious beyond that horizon. It's true that there had been anticipation in the early years, but now even that seemed to have dropped away. All that was left was a profoundly calm sense of freedom. It was as if he had given up everything already, and then when death had proven elusive, given up on death too. "I'm just beginning to experience a taste of what I was speaking of, all those years," he told me. "This is the period of my primary growth. Just *being* in this state." After so much skill with stillness, so deep a knowledge of silence, he had found an even deeper level of quietude.

Like so many other religious leaders throughout history, the Buddha taught the wisdom of an intimate familiarity with death. Monks are instructed to practice in charnel grounds and to visualize the stages of decay of a human corpse in vivid detail. The most ordinary practices for laypeople include daily reminders of death's imminence and its unknowable schedule. Death is the great motivator: Your time here is short; use it well! Death is the unavoidable, irrevocable proof of the logic of impermanence: You will not last; no one you love will last, so you'd best loosen your grip and walk more lightly through this temporary existence. Christianity has its own tradition of memento mori, though it has been buried in the modern American practice of concealing death's reality and our discomfort with it behind a wall of cosmetic denial and evasion. As a Benedictine monk, Thomas embraced death fearlessly.

If I am lucky, I would hope to find the same fearlessness in the face of death that I saw in him. I'm grateful to have had the chance to observe it closely; there is no better teaching. It was not the fearlessness of defying death or conquering it; there was no such bluster in it. Nor was it a fearlessness that implies an absence of sadness and loss. Human emotions are not erased from the experience, and I miss him dearly. The infusions of heart remain present; they just don't hold the power to sway the mind off-center.

CHAPTER 14

Forgiveness

.

.

.

I tell you this
to break your heart,
by which I mean only
that it break open and never close again
to the rest of the world.

—MARY OLIVER

The raw stone walls and the blue light filtering through stained-glass windows made the chapel a cave-like sanctuary. I often went to the small Episcopal monastery of the Cowley Fathers to find a space of silence in the day. It was the only place I could find, aside from the library where the smell of book mold was unpleasant, that offered some respite from the urban clamor of Cambridge and from Harvard's departmental politicking. It wasn't just the silence that drew me. I took pleasure in being there during the prayers and liturgy too, which is how I one day found myself standing next to a small, elderly black man who turned to me when it came time to offer the exchange, "Peace be with you." His face and his twinkling grin were familiar, but given the slightly incongruous tracksuit he was wearing I couldn't quite place him. Then he introduced himself with the humility of consummate understatement, "I'm Tutu. I used to be the archbishop of Cape Town."

We chatted after the service. My maroon robes were familiar to him and he laughed gleefully remembering his meetings with the Dalai Lama. The other Nobel laureates could keep their gravitas; these two provoked each other to a silly goofiness. I learned he was in the United States on sabbatical and would be teaching at the Episcopal Divinity School about his experience with South Africa's truth and reconciliation process. As it happened, I was already taking the course there, which was co-taught by the renowned feminist theologian Reverend Carter Heyward.

Sometimes teachers appear without fanfare or mystery, without even much of a personal connection, but simply taking their place at the front of a classroom, talking about what they have come to know. However mundane and institutional the framing, the lessons may still be profound, and the teacher's presence still a living embodiment of the lesson. When that presence shines with such offhand humility as Archbishop Desmond Tutu's, it's a good reminder that no one here is especially unique.

In class, Tutu spoke of the challenges he faced as the head of South Africa's Truth and Reconciliation Commission, which investigated the abuses of the apartheid regime that had held power through legalized cruelty, humiliation, and violence both secretive and blatant, as well as the answering violence that the anti-apartheid movement was eventually driven to. When Nelson Mandela, as the former prisoner and new president of a country that was emerging from what amounted to a negotiated revolution, invited his jailer to his inauguration as a guest of honor, he set the tone for a stunning invitation to forgiveness. When Mandela asked Tutu to lead the commission, his choice was an acknowledgment that the work that needed to be done was spiritual as well as political, legal, and psychological. The commission's mandate was not to punish the perpetrators but to promote healing, both on an individual and societal level, of the wounds inflicted by a racist and unjust system. Their task was to begin to reconcile a divided country where blacks and whites had lived for generations as oppressed and oppressors, and had been driven to the brink of civil war. Now that the tables had turned, the black majority held democratically elected power for the first time, but the wounds were deep and still very raw. The fear was that a wave of violent retribution would undo the precarious moral victory.

Given the goal of reconciliation, the commission needed to avoid revenge disguised as victor's justice or the rigidity of the normal criminal justice process that, given the scale of the offenses, would be so painfully prolonged that it would forestall healing. A blanket amnesty that would have left the culture of impunity unshaken was also rejected. The commission devised a process that focused first on truth-telling, gathering some twenty thousand statements where both victims and perpetrators attested to abductions, killings, torture, and other gross violations of human rights. Roughly one in ten of those were invited to give testimony at public hearings with saturated media coverage. Those perpetrators who offered a full confession, which was then verified, were granted amnesty. A system of reparations for the victims was also established.

The intended purpose of the truth-telling was accountability, an antidote to the secrecy and repression of the apartheid regime's police state. The public airing of the stories also offered a profound catharsis, a restoration of dignity, and closure for grieving families who until then had been unable to learn how their loved ones had disappeared, or to bury their dead. Most striking of all, and a surprise to many, was how the truth-telling kindled an impulse to forgiveness. When a person confesses a painful truth, expresses remorse, and is heard, the acts of speaking and hearing have a power to forge bonds of heartfelt human connection.

Forgiveness was not a universal response to the truth-telling. For many it was out of reach, and it certainly could not be taken for granted. And yet that transformation was surprisingly common. Time and again, there was a remarkable showing of the strength that inheres within human vulnerability.

The systematic program of torture, killing, and humiliation that enforced apartheid required that the perpetrators see their opponents as less than human. The racism that was apartheid's rationale only amplified that dehumanization. In the process the enforcers themselves were dehumanized by their own brutality. When a perpetrator finds the empathy to take a victim's perspective and feel remorse, they have taken the first step on a journey that can restore their own humanity. The victim's impulse to forgive is a meeting halfway on that journey. By exercising the power to accept that offering of remorse, a victim reclaims their own agency and the dignity that was stripped from them. At that meeting point, the humanity that was damaged on both sides begins to heal.

While listening to Tutu describe the heartrending encounters that the commission's framework had enabled, it became clear that forgiveness was not just a fluffy sentimental notion, but a life-changing tool that could move relationships toward reconciliation. I was struck by the intricate mesh between such personal moments of spiritual transformation and the larger public project of restorative justice as a remedy for a traumatized society. Most surprising of all, forgiveness was in some unlikely sense scalable; it had a role in policy. Obviously, you couldn't compel it, and you couldn't allow it to justify abuse or let harm stand without correction. But perhaps you could create the conditions and space for forgiveness, the catalysts that would promote this healing chemistry.

The Truth and Reconciliation Commission that Tutu led was far from a complete or flawless solution for South Africa's needs. Now, two decades later, it has been criticized especially for the inadequacy of reparations that failed to correct systemic inequalities. But it was a remarkably effective response to the uncertainties and urgent needs of the time. After the commission had wrapped up its work, Tutu traveled to Rwanda, Ireland and Northern Ireland, Israel and Palestine to share the lessons the commission had learned. It could serve as a model, although not in every detail because they were learning as they went along, and because the process as designed was finely tuned to the specific conditions of the time and place.

Nelson Mandela once said that if Tutu had not been involved, the truth and reconciliation process would have failed miserably. The archbishop clearly brought extraordinary personal and spiritual resources to bear on that moment of history. I don't think that age diminished the man I came to admire. His very presence seemed evidence that Tutu had the balance of contemplative and active life down to an art. His energy seemed to spring from a bottomless source, and was fully charged whether he was addressing a crowd or in the quiet of a private meeting. He talked about how he had been looking forward to retirement, expecting to celebrate the end of apartheid with a time of hard-earned rest, only to be summoned to more than two intense years of high-stakes work that would daily drain the emotional resources of all involved. Even when that was over he hardly paused. During his so-called sabbatical in the United States, he was still down in the dirt, fighting for gay and lesbian rights, for indigenous people's rights in Canada and the United States, and for Palestinian rights at a time when very few were willing to risk raising their voices.

Though he expressed himself passionately in a very strong voice, I never heard any shadow of resentment cross that voice. He wasn't shy to speak in anger, but the fires of his anger burned clean. They didn't seem to be fueled by his own personal suffering or any grudge. It is rare to meet anger that carries no taint of hate, no effort to dehumanize a target, and that fascinated me. I'm convinced that his energy, and his capacity for forgiveness, are gifts that flow from his contemplative practice.

Prayer, and his daily celebration of the Eucharist, seemed the most natural of disciplines. Prayer was for him a discipline in the sense that eating and bathing regularly are acts of discipline. He didn't elevate his spiritual practice above anything else in his daily routine, but he would not have neglected it any more than he would abandon any other basic task of living.

There is a deeper discipline to contemplative life that Tutu embodied as well. The daily repetition of formal practice—be it prayer or meditation or any contemplative exercise of the mind and heart—is a way of building a skill. The purpose of the repetition is to internalize the skills so thoroughly that they kick in automatically when we need them. We put the practice into practice. The fruits of that kind of discipline manifest most obviously when things go wrong. How we respond to adversity is the measure of how deeply integrated our practice is. The ability to forgive those who have harmed us, genuinely and generously, is a test passed with flying colors.

Forgiveness receives far less attention in Buddhism than it does in Christianity, where so much flows from the idea of God's forgiveness of humans' sins. The Buddha taught that the karmic consequences of wrongdoing—or doing good— are simply effects that arise from causes. Our actions lay down imprints in our stream of consciousness that form tendencies and have impacts beyond the immediately obvious. The chain of cause and effect may be as subtle and difficult to track as the currents from the butterfly wings that set off a tornado on the other side of the earth. Or the harm we cause may be obvious—and available to our remorse and efforts at correction. There is no judgment in the Christian sense, no divine retribution, only the workings of a natural law. Tradition and custom have laid down pathways: We confess harmful actions, express remorse, and ask for forgiveness of the teacher or of enlightened beings. There is a ritual in the monastic community for dealing with transgressions that break vows, where the superior council acknowledges your remorse and may advise on a course correction. But there is oddly little emphasis on asking forgiveness of a person you have harmed, or offering forgiveness to someone who has harmed you, and I had not given it much thought before Tutu's example centered the idea in my mind.

There is one very well-known story from the Buddha's life where forgiveness is a crucial theme, though hardly spelled out. Angulimala was an infamous highway brigand, a killer who set himself to the grisly task of collecting one finger from each of a thousand victims. He stole nothing else from them, but strung the severed fingers into a necklace that he wore around his neck. By the time he crossed paths with the Buddha, he had already taken 999 lives, compelled whole villages to be abandoned in fear, and caused untold suffering. Instead of becoming the thousandth victim, the Buddha invited him— fearlessly, calmly, and without anger—to stop killing and terrorizing, and to become a monk. Instead of turning Angulimala in to the authorities, the Buddha ordained him, to the community's extreme consternation. When he joined the monks on begging rounds and people recognized him and stoned him, his only reaction was to ask for forgiveness. And, to the surprise of his fellow monks, his enlightenment came swiftly.

The Buddha saw the particular efficacy of a solution that sheltered the criminal within the community rather than ostracizing him, however shocking that seemed both to the families of his victims and to the other monks. And no doubt the Buddha also saw that the other monks had something to learn from the situation. Of course, the gesture could have failed. The story would be remembered differently if, after being ordained, Angulimala had chopped off a fellow monk's finger. There was something about the Buddha's fearless acceptance, his unflinching forgiveness, that created an opportunity for a villain to recall his better self and begin a transformation. It's not that Angulimala's change was instantaneous and miraculous. The story makes no claim that a miracle was involved, beyond the strangely unbounded nature of human potential.

As a civic society today, we lack the gestures and the vocabulary, institutionally and otherwise, to offer forgiveness and invite the transformation that it enables. We may take pride in standing up against capital punishment, but we don't have the courage to embrace and accept convicted criminals as individuals and honor their potential as human beings. We may warm to a story of redemption when Hollywood has processed it for us, but we haven't designed our penal system with redemption as a possibility, let alone a goal. For want of a practical map that centers the restoration of human dignity, we have abdicated our own role in constituting the community that could provide a healing environment. The result is the profit-driven gulag that is mass incarceration in the United States today.

There is a practical role for forgiveness in the criminal justice system, not just from individuals but from society as a whole. Europe has begun to explore methods of restorative justice that turn away from punitive vengeance and give priority instead to a victim's restitution and a criminal's rehabilitation. The criminal remains first and foremost a human being, and a measure of success is when that human being is assimilated back into society as a normal citizen. In the United States, a felon is branded for life, shutting the door to many opportunities that would support rehabilitation. It's a twisted, vengeful form of justice for a nation that claims "in God we trust." It's particularly hellish for many whom the legal system has failed with wrongful convictions that destroy innocent lives.

When a society tries to rebuild itself after suffering trauma on a national scale, like South Africa and others that have worked with truth and reconciliation processes after the anguish of a civil war or a revolution, there is a need for legal frameworks that include forgiveness on an institutional as well as an individual level. It would be well for the United States to acknowledge its own traumatic history of slavery and genocide, and consider the need for a process that makes forgiveness and healing possible. Amnesty should not be just a rubber stamp that allows someone who plays by the rules to get off scot-free. It should instead offer a path for an individual who has done harm to become a better human being.

In a complex human environment, asking and giving forgiveness are essential behavioral tools that can move beyond shame and remorse to enable healing. Forgiveness seems a natural complement to the core Buddhist practices that cultivate compassion and loving-kindness. When we practice extending compassion equally in all directions—to those we love, to those we feel neutral toward, and to those we perceive as our enemies—forgiveness is a missing link in the exercise. In practical terms, we need to forgive those who have harmed us or who seem hateful to us before we can genuinely feel compassion or loving-kindness toward them. In the absence of forgiveness, generating goodwill toward those from whom we instinctively recoil remains a brittle, cerebral game, or else a transactional calculation of return.

The purpose of such practices is not just a flexing of the heart muscles that will make compassion and loving-kindness arise more spontaneously, but also a leveling of our natural biases. Of course it's easier to extend our hearts to an inner circle of friends and family. We are biologically programmed to do so. It's much more challenging to embrace strangers with equal warmth. If we can learn to see our erstwhile enemies through the same lens of compassion and love, we will be loosening our tight claw hold on the illusion that our enemies are made of different stuff than ourselves, or that anyone is inherently an enemy. At the same time, we will have made a concrete step toward dismantling the tribalism that plagues the human race.

The instant we identify someone as an enemy, the psychology of bias runs predictable scripts in our minds. What until then was a neutral figure, not fully defined and still open to interpretation, hardens into a two-dimensional caricature, its outlines penned thick and black, isolating it from context. We see a villain, unchanging and irredeemable, rather than a complex human being, fallible and perhaps terribly flawed but with the potential to change and grow. In the reinforced bubbles of lives submerged in media, that psychology of bias is further exaggerated. The adversary becomes a narcissist or a sociopath, hell-bent on destroying our world. We are roiled to defend ourselves against alien rapists or vile racists. Or perhaps we congratulate ourselves that we have a more sophisticated view. We recognize that the evil adversary is systemic, rooted in history, a tangled web of past causes and current incentives. But when we are under attack, in the adrenaline-charged moment it's hard to hold all that complexity aloft. We compress and abbreviate to sight a target, and once again we are tilting full speed ahead at a caricature.

In our eagerness to right wrongs, we project our own flaws in ways that sabotage the work of compassion and social justice. Subtle investments of ego cling to our most idealistic efforts and undermine them. However discreetly, we see ourselves as heroes and saviors. We wear haloes under our hats. Always, we are in the driver's seat. We charge ahead to meet the enemy, but as long as our own minds are clouded and agitated, we inevitably fog the lens. We not only see more chaos in the world, we contribute to it. That filter means we don't even get an accurate diagnosis of the problems, whether inside us or out in the world, to be able to change effectively.

Here is where learning to be nonjudgmental shows its true value, though its meaning in Buddhism has so often been misunderstood in the West. Being nonjudgmental does not mean giving up discernment. It does not mean ignoring injustice, cozying up to corruption, or viewing the complexities of an ethical gray scale through fluffy pink clouds. In Buddhist terms, being nonjudgmental was originally part of training to suspend one's own projections and biases. The goal was never to turn a blind eye, but to see more clearly without distortion. Here too forgiveness may have a role to play, because it demands that we see the darkness clearly before moving toward reconciliation. The truth portion of "truth and reconciliation" cannot be skipped. There can be no genuine forgiveness, or any other correction, without first acknowledging that something was wrong. Nor does forgiving mean forgetting. Holding in memory the truth of harm done is crucial to preventing that harm from being repeated, but we can forgive even as we say, "Never again!"

If we really want to change the world, transforming ourselves—recognizing that we too are part of that world—is a necessary part of getting the job done. We share others' faults in ways that are hard for us to see ourselves. This is not an argument for quietism, spiritual bypassing, or accepting wrongdoing passively. Nor is contemplative practice a luxury or indulgence as popular notions of self-care sometimes suggest. Contemplative practice is essential nourishment that fuels the active life. The familiar tension that pits Martha against Mary, the one who serves actively against the contemplative, is a false binary. There is a powerful synergy between those two ways of being in the world, and each can fail without the other. Any kind of contemplative discipline that begins to shift your heart and mind can unlock a reservoir of motivation, compassion, and wisdom to channel where it is needed. Without that inner work, rage against the injustice of the world and fatigue at the never-ending nature of the task make a toxic mix that leads to burnout and sours compassion into cynicism. If you truly begin to change yourself, it becomes much easier to change the world around you, and to do so without throwing even more anger and divisiveness into the stew.

And yet, an essential part of what it takes to transform ourselves is the desire to transform the world: *If one wishes to have inner peace one must first pray for peace in the four directions.* We cannot sit quietly and pray in a burning house. An individual who seeks inner peace has a spiritual responsibility to create the conditions for peace in the world. If the conflagration of the world's suffering does not move us to compassion, then the spiritual path will wind in circles around us and lead nowhere.

The redemptive forgiveness that Archbishop Tutu hoped to awaken in his terribly damaged country was conceived as a mirror of God's forgiveness of humankind's sins, because his Christian faith is anchored in the idea that all of humanity is created in God's image. A Buddhist might point instead to the essential Buddha nature that every sentient being possesses—the potential that exists in all conscious life to awaken into an unclouded view of reality, to see the truth of our infinitely interrelated existence. The stories we weave, the mechanisms we conceive, are fundamentally different, but they point to the same underlying reality. If you can keep in sight that promise of the redemptive potential of our very existence, the hard work of forgiveness and healing becomes easier.

CHAPTER 15

Sierra Nevada de Santa Marta, Colombia, 2014

·
·
·

I find that somehow, by shifting the focus of attention, I become the very thing I look at, and experience the kind of consciousness it has; I become the inner witness of the thing. I call this capacity of entering other focal points of consciousness, love; you may give it any name you like. Love says "I am everything." Wisdom says "I am nothing." Between the two, my life flows. Since at any point of time and space I can be both the subject and the object of experience, I express it by saying that I am both, and neither, and beyond both.

—NISARGADATTA

The views were of vast, distant peaks dusted with snow, clouds curling their fingers into the valleys below us. The sky seemed just inches above our heads, the air brilliant. The silence was a honed edge broken only by our footsteps.

This region of the Sierra Nevada de Santa Marta, the mountain range that towers above Colombia's northern coast, is sacred to the indigenous Arhuaco people. They do not allow outsiders who don't appreciate the significance of these mountains, where the creation of the universe began, to use the trails we were walking. The fact that we were there was a mark of their trust. I still had no idea why I was there; all I knew was that they had asked me to come.

I had been invited to Colombia to speak to the faculty of the Universidad Del Rosario in Bogotá about the work that I was doing at MIT with the Dalai Lama Center for Ethics and Transformative Values. Del Rosario has been at the heart of Colombia's political as well as cultural life for three and a half centuries, and a great many of the country's leaders, both historically and today, are alumni. The university was interested in the experiential learning pedagogy in ethics and peace building that the Center had developed at MIT, and we were beginning to explore how it might be adapted to the particular challenges that Colombia faced.

One generally knows what to expect at academic meetings of that nature. What I did not expect was the message that the dean conveyed to me. He seemed as surprised by it as I was. A delegation of Arhuacos had arrived from the mountains, sent by their leaders, known as Mamos. They are elders who are trained from childhood in a complex cosmology and intimate understanding of the natural and spiritual worlds that guide their decisions on all aspects of their community's life.

The Arhuacos' isolation might suggest a primitive tribal culture but in fact they, along with three neighboring groups that are closely related, are a substantial remnant of a continuous civilization that survived the Spanish conquest. They have also survived every intrusion into their territory since

then: the continuous encroachment of settlers from the low-
lands, the clearing of forests for the marijuana trade and then
for cocaine, and the violence that followed in the wake of
these crops, including violence to the land—the laying of land
mines to protect the crops, the spraying of fields to eradicate
the crops—and the shifting factions of guerrillas, military,
and paramilitary. With each new incursion the indigenous
people have been forced higher into the more inaccessible,
and less productive, reaches of their mountain range. Secrecy
and isolation have for centuries been part of their strategy for
preserving their culture, but in recent years they have also
learned to work proactively with Colombia's legal system and
international organizations to advocate for their rights and
environmental protections.

Apparently an elder Mamo had a dream that someone they
needed to talk to could be found just then in Bogotá, someone
who had come from the East and wore red cloth. The university was their connection to civilization, so that's where they
sent the message. The dean put two and two together. No one
else fit the description. Would I be willing to meet with them?
The Mamos never leave their sacred territory in the mountains, so we would have to go there. The dean was reluctant
to impose, he said, because our schedule was tight and the
journey to the Sierra Nevada de Santa Marta would be no
simple matter, but since the messengers themselves had come
all the way to Bogotá . . .

This was how I found myself on this path walking through
an extraordinarily beautiful mountain landscape, accompanied by Dean Eduardo Barajas Sandoval, the Arhuaco messengers, and a handful of faculty members. There was an
anthropologist, Angela Santamaria, who had been studying
the Arhuaco for many years; Patricia Acosta, a professor of

urban studies and planning whom I had met when she was on a fellowship to MIT; and Raul Velasquez, a professor of political science who was extremely skeptical of this bizarre diversion from the work we had planned but was intrigued enough to join the expedition.

The trip was indeed daunting. We flew from Bogotá to Valledupar, and from there we drove for several hours up into the mountains. The road became less and less of a road, dissolving into a rocky track that edged ravines and cliff faces and crossed rivers that were fortunately shallow at that time of year. Nabusímake was the end of the road, as far as vehicles were concerned. This was the spiritual center of the Arhuaco universe, the spot where the sun was originally born from the realm of pure thought. It is also the site of the Capuchin mission that worked hard to erase the old culture, until the Arhuacos rose up and expelled the friars in the 1980s. The village, with its mud houses roofed in steep thatch and gardens like small forests of fruiting trees, now seems barely touched by the modern world. It is idyllically quiet, absent of the noise of engines and amplified media that would be crackling in the background of an Indian village today.

From Nabusímake we walked. We left behind paddocks enclosed by low stone walls and hiked deeper into the mountains for almost three hours, the path alternately dipping into forest and then opening to broad slopes of grassy alpine meadows. I hadn't come to Colombia prepared for hiking, and the only shoes I had brought were deemed inadequate defense against mud and snakes. Some rubber boots were found that almost fit, but after hours of walking my shins were rubbed raw.

We finally arrived at a compound with a few thatched huts. I gathered that the Mamos were inside, but before we could enter the area, the Arhuacos who had accompanied us from Bogotá said we should sit and prepare ourselves. So we sat on the rocks nearby, quiet with anticipation. The only sound was of each man softly tapping a stick on the small gourd that he carried at all times, rotating it around and around. From time to time they would dip the stick into the gourd and then into their mouths, mixing lime with the coca leaves they were chewing. The handling of the gourd, all the tapping and turning, was said to increase their wisdom. The motion and sound, and its constant presence, reminded me of prayer wheels in the hands of elderly Tibetans.

We sat like this for more than an hour. Some women came out of the compound and sat with us quietly, and then a handful of older men came and welcomed us. They tied a knotted thread made of agave fiber around my wrist, the same agave fiber that their domed white hats were made of, which were said to represent the snow-covered peaks of the mountain range. The men each carried a woven bag of agave fiber with a pattern unique to their family. They all wore the simplest clothes, all more or less identical, of a homespun white cloth.

We then walked a slight distance from the compound to what they called a sacred hill, where the meeting would take place. The anthropologist confided that she felt a little envious, and puzzled too. In all her years of working with the Arhuaco, they had never invited her into that area. The three Mamos were sitting in front of a round hut made of straw. They wore the same homespun white clothes, the same snow-cap hats as the other Arhuaco men, and there was nothing that marked their authority beyond advanced age and a certain gravitas in their bearing. I asked if there was any specific ritual for entering the space. I noticed that the Mamos were barefoot, and I mentioned that in India we would never enter a holy place without taking off our shoes. Everybody agreed that it would be a good idea if it wasn't inconvenient. I was only too happy to ditch the rubber boots and let my feet feel the earth.

We all sat quietly again for a while on wooden stools and flat stones set in front of the hut. Once again the only sound was our own breathing and the gentle tapping of sticks on gourds, with the Mamos now joining in too. And then, without introduction, Guneymaku Chaparro began talking. He was the eldest of the three, perhaps in his midseventies, though it was hard to tell age on skin made leathery by the high-altitude sun.

Chaparro spoke in an indigenous language that everyone referred to generically as *lengua*. He led the conversation and the other Mamos joined in intermittently. One of the younger Arhuacos translated into Spanish, and my companions then translated from Spanish into English for my sake. At least that was how it started. Chaparro began by answering the question that had followed me all the way from Bogotá: Why on earth was I here? He explained that three hundred years ago they had received a prophecy of sorts, a legend that looked to the future rather than the past, saying that someone would come from the East, wearing red cloth, and that they should share wisdom with this person. He had had a dream indicating that the person they were waiting for had come to the city, and so they had sent their representatives to Bogotá to bring me here.

As the translation came through, Eduardo gave me a look that said, "This is insane!" And yet I could also see that he was moved by the setting and the seriousness of the encounter. The Mamos explained that they had stayed awake all the previous night, out in the open, in preparation for our meeting. They looked a little tired—it was now almost evening again—but not as tired as I would be at half their age. They had spent the hours, they said, asking for guidance from nature and from particular spirits as to how they should welcome me and what they should discuss.

I thanked them for inviting me. I didn't want to probe the story of the prophecy. It seemed more worthwhile to focus instead on whatever it was that they wanted to share with me. Chaparro began to speak about relationships. What he expressed carried a profound sorrow. He was grieving for his brothers in the outside world who had lost something terribly precious. That loss was as hard as a death, and so he was mourning, because what they had lost was the very nature of how to be human: an understanding of how to be in relationship.

He spoke of the Arhuacos' relationship with this land, about their responsibility as guardians of the health and harmony of these mountains and how the mountains were a mother that had so unselfishly provided for their needs. That relationship he described as the original law, and all of their understanding of nature evolved from relationship. It was not only this region they knew so well and their own needs that mattered. Because the entire universe was first created right here, in the Sierra Nevada de Santa Marta, the health of this region was key to the survival and health of the whole world.

The Arhuacos perceive the world as a single living body, the rivers and streams its veins and arteries. The health of this body consists in a precarious and dynamic balance—a literal homeostasis of the organism—that the Mamos are responsible for monitoring and for mending when needed. Even the most mundane activity, life by its very nature, the taking of a breath, the eating of a meal, a birth or a death, shifts the balance in subtle ways. A dispute in the village, an illness, an accident, a family torn by jealousy—these are ailments in the organism, strains in relationship that the Mamos tend to with care. Building a dam is like blocking an artery. Traditionally, when the health of the system is threatened, they repair the natural order through spiritual work, through guidance in the community, and making ritual "payments." The destruction they were witnessing today, the selfishness of their brothers in the cities, the hatred and killing they inflicted on one another, and the extraction of resources from their mother's body, all shifted the balance catastrophically, beyond the capacity of the Mamos' powers to correct. The messages from nature that they intercepted foretold much worse to come: the threat of the oceans flooding the land and the sun burning the earth barren.

At some point in the conversation I became aware that we had left behind our support system of trilingual translation. Chaparro was speaking in the indigenous *lengua* and I was speaking English. The understanding was immediate and instantaneous and we were responding to each other without waiting for the translators who trailed behind us. What I heard in the Mamo's voice and read in the shadows that crossed his face was a deeply empathic concern for the suffering that this failure of relationship had caused. "These mountains, they are in pain," he said. He spoke gently, but with emotion as tender and raw as if his own child or sister or mother was dying. The relationship he was pointing to was real, not metaphor.

◦

Walking back to Nabusímake, I was processing all of this. I was walking slowly, the rubber boots once again a torment. Raul, the professor of political science who had been so skeptical on the journey out, kindly held back to keep pace with me. He too needed to process, having shed his skepticism in favor of a free-flowing elation, and his processing was verbal. Finally I said, "Raul, would you mind just enjoying the nature and walking silently together?" He offered instead, "Would you mind if I play Tchaikovsky?" It was a good compromise, so the transcendent views and the weight of the Mamos' message had a cinematic soundtrack from his phone for the remainder of our hike.

The very brief glimpse I had into the Mamos' world shook me profoundly. It had not occurred to me that there are ways of relating to nature that are far beyond the realm of my own experience. I've had the benefit of an excellent education in the natural sciences, long periods of contemplative solitude in nature, and the pleasure of countless hours spent framing nature's glorious displays through a camera's eye. None of this prepared me for what the Mamos were trying to communicate. I have deep-rooted memories of my own family's ties to the land of Vaishali, the quiet bond that elders shared with the earthen goddess Bhu Devi, and the practical rhythms of farming life. But compared to the pulsing umbilical cord that links the Mamos to the Sierra Nevada de Santa Marta, our ties to the land are attenuated. We have divided our attention for generations.

And yet I remember as a child watching an elderly man planting saplings in our village. These would be mango trees one day, he said, and I was eager to know how long that would take. It would take three or four years, he said, before the first fruit appeared. But the fruit of the first year was never very good, so maybe in five years the mangoes would be ready to enjoy. That seemed a very long time indeed—I was maybe seven or eight years old myself, so it was most of a lifetime.

"Baba, how old are you?" I asked.

His smile bared a single tooth hanging from his gum. "I am ninety-two years old!" he said proudly.

"Baba, will you still be here to enjoy the mangoes?"

"I won't, but you will be." He was more than content, even proud, to invest his efforts in a future that wasn't his own. He had the same leathered skin, and wore the same kind of white homespun cloth, work-stained and sun-bleached, that the Arhuacos wore, and his face had appeared to my mind's eye for a moment as I listened to Chaparro. The unselfishly long view that both those men embodied should not seem mysterious to us. Every day we reap the benefits of previous generations' foresight, but we seem to have lost that faculty ourselves.

The Mamos' view of relationships made a profound impression on me. Their own self-interest and their very urgent concerns for their own people seemed secondary to a larger, holistic concern for the whole world. It was a concern that was practical, grounded in the most fundamental of physical needs and a livelihood of bare sustenance. And yet it was also a transcendent and unselfish expression of love, shining in contrast with the way that our own relationships—and not just our relationship with nature—lean toward the transactional. Our culture has taught us to weave meaning and magic around relationships that mask the reductive calculations we make consciously or unconsciously. We can become entranced by rituals of reciprocity and the satisfying dance of give and take. We spin stories about how these relationships are loving and deeply caring, but the roles we play are rarely as selfless as the stories would have us believe. At the end of the day, love that is truly offered freely shakes off the bonds of self-interest and self-cherishing. However it begins, it moves beyond the constraints of a transactional, calculating mindset.

Bodhicitta—that impulse that draws us toward enlightenment—offers a clear-sighted view that cuts through the stories and sees into the deeper nature of reality. It sees who we are as sentient beings and understands that we are capable of purely loving, caring relationships, where nothing is expected in return. Nothing is even hoped for, except for others' well-being. There are those who claim that such unselfishness is impossible, that even if we expect nothing in this lifetime, we have simply offloaded our expectations of reward to an afterlife. They insist we are still checking the balance of our account even if the merit is supposedly spiritual. They have never imagined themselves in the seat of an archetypal Bodhisattva. Avalokiteshvara, the Bodhisattva of compassion, is not worried about his next lifetime, or a merit-driven higher rebirth. He's made the choice to stay behind, available in this life until we are all enlightened, and not one sentient being is left behind. That is not a finite task. We won't become Bodhisattvas unless we learn to identify and abandon motives rooted in transactional calculation, to practice cherishing others more dearly than ourselves, and to extend the same openhearted compassion and unselfish love to all human beings equally, including those far outside our natural circles of affinity.

Why not extend the boundaries of unselfish relationship beyond other humans, beyond even the handful of animals who appeal to our anthropomorphic imaginations? Suppose we could expand our circle of care to encompass all forms of life and the whole of the environment? I would care for a tree not because it has some utilitarian function, giving me shade, food, timber; not even because it's beautiful and I desire the pleasure of gazing on this tree. There is a different kind of pleasure, call it an "aesthetics of relationship," that appreci-

ates the larger whole in which the tree and I are equally par-
ticipants. We understand how objectifying another person
dehumanizes them, makes them less than they are. Can we
learn in the same spirit not to objectify a tree?

This aesthetic response to a more holistic view of our relationship with nature begins with the premise that we are all
interconnected. We recognize that we need one another for
our survival. Yes, we have needs and desires, but we don't
translate our needs and desires into utilitarian models that
become a filter for perception and assigning value. Instead we
recognize that because we are interconnected, our sense of
well-being—our health and wholeness, the very integrity of
our existence—is tied to the health and wholeness of other
beings. That sense of profound interconnection might sound
like a naïve and romantic projection, but the fact is that other
models haven't worked well for us. The way we have framed
the world thus far tends to devolve to exploitation and op-
pression.

•

By the time we reached the village, I was eager to wash. There
was no indoor running water. Instead, our Arhuaco companions showed me to a shallow stream and gave me a lesson.
There was no container to collect or pour water, and no need
for one. You lay down flat on your back and let the stream
run over you, then turned over and lay on your stomach while
the stream washed over your back. Soap up and repeat to
rinse off. It was icy cold but it was effortless, and there was
something in the molding of one's body to the stream bed, the
melting of resistance into the melted snow, that seemed to
echo the Mamos' message.

I returned from Bogotá to MIT as if I were carrying home

a most precious and fragile living cargo. What the Mamos did by reaching out and asking me to hear them felt like a profound gift of trust. That relationship brought with it responsibility.

There was a big conference in the works and the Dalai Lama would be participating. The theme was a global view of ethics and a long-term view of ethical responsibility as a framework for addressing climate change and the array of challenges that will ensue. VUCA is the label that the corporate world has borrowed from military jargon to describe the state of this world: volatile, uncertain, complex, ambiguous. In practical terms, a long view of ethics and our responsibility to future generations is the only path that makes sense in the time we have left to act. But a long view also matters in spiritual terms. Right now whatever energy we are putting into staving off environmental catastrophe is driven by fear. It's a usefully motivating fear, to be sure, but fear by its nature is selfish. If we had a true understanding of our intimate ties to all other human beings and to the natural world—the understanding of relationship that the Mamos embodied, our actions would be driven instead by a deep sense of love—not by fear but our care for this vast family.

I dedicated that meeting to the Mamos and told their story, which is now part of the story of the Dalai Lama Center for Ethics and Transformative Values at MIT. I tried to explain to His Holiness who these people were that had so inspired me. Their way of life was even simpler, I told him, much simpler than the Tibetan nomads had lived traditionally. I wasn't sure he understood until I gave him the gift they had asked me to give to my teacher: one knotted strand of agave fiber, just like the one they had tied on my wrist. That simple piece of string was as humble and as precious a gift as the thread that Khunu

Lama had pulled from his fraying coat, and it conveyed a similar message: The truest blessing is that we are tied together. We are small threads woven together into a vast web. Nothing has value in isolation. Even our transactional calculations of what seems valuable here and now are narrow intimations of a deeper truth—that our only value and purpose is in relationship to one another, if we could only stop counting the threads and see the glorious patterns in this intricate and infinite fabric.

I wake up every day with the memory of my teachers' compassion, with the joy and wisdom that so many remarkable individuals have shared with me, and I ask myself how I can manifest that same compassion in action. Talking about it doesn't seem to be enough. The real challenge is not the ever-escalating threat of change. Change always looms, if rarely so dramatically as now. The real challenge is to bring this scattered family together, to reach across the boundaries of our separate beliefs, with empathy and a shared understanding of ethics, to learn to care for one another.

EPILOGUE

.
.
.

"Do you remember how I used to give you trouble for borrowing my shoes?"

"Yes, when we wore the same size." I could picture the shoes lined up near the door, slipping them on as I left for school. Because I could, because they fit. My father had impeccable taste, and a teenage boy didn't think ahead to how a sudden scuffle or impromptu game might not return those finely crafted and costly shoes in the same condition. "I'll bring you a new pair, something special, when I come to Delhi next. I can't borrow your shoes anymore, my own feet have grown."

"It's not only your feet that have outgrown my shoes. You've outgrown me altogether." There was a flush in his voice that carried down the phone line, all the way from Delhi to Cambridge. Now that my parents were aging, I made a point of calling regularly on weekends. Our conversations were usually light and casual, but on this particular beautiful fall morning my father went off on a sentimental tangent. "You're thirty-two years old. When I was your age, I had just finished university and started teaching. But I had never even left Bihar. You've traveled the world. You've done so much good work that I really admire and appreciate. You have become a teacher to the world."

The emotional tone was entirely familiar, his own effusive style, but I was stunned to be on the receiving end of this observation. Never would I have expected to hear that phrase, "a teacher to the world," from his mouth. I stood in the kitchen, phone in hand and tears welling up. I was running late—we had been talking for half an hour—but I couldn't bring myself to end the conversation.

It was one of the last times I talked with my father before he died. Neither of us were seeking closure in the sense that that term is used in the West. Neither of us had picked up the phone with an agenda. In recent years we had reached what felt like an understanding, though not acceptance, of each other's position, and I didn't hope for more than that. What happened between us on the phone that day was entirely unexpected, and yet it emerged as effortlessly and spontaneously as my encounters with teachers that I've described in this book.

We spend so much of our lives seeking others' validation and permission for the choices and decisions we make. We long for those whose opinions we value to recognize us, to see our journey. But engaging with mystery, and the peculiar chemistry of how that manifests in human connection, is something that happens in its own time, on its own terms. That is a stark truth that we have no choice but to face. All we can do is be open and ready to embrace it when it comes.

I would like to think that this book is not just about me.

I'm not different from countless other seekers in the past, and the future too, who have chosen to embrace the mystery that beckons them and to follow where it leads. I hope you will see some part of yourself mirrored in my story and I encourage you, with joyful enthusiasm, to embark on your own contemplative journey toward self-actualization.

I respectfully urge you who study the mystery,
don't pass your days and nights in vain.

—SEKITO KISEN

ACKNOWLEDGMENTS

A monk's life by definition is a recognition of the interconnected and interdependent reality that underlies all things, even if they seem disconnected. This attempt to reflect part of my spiritual life in a book is a culmination of the efforts and kindness of many individuals across the world, too many to mention by name but all objects of my gratitude in my daily remembrances. I include M.Y. and R.H. for their generous friendship, Ella and Wayne Wu for their continued support, my sisters, Shefali and Shilpa, who have always been supportive of my risky explorations, and my mother, who learned to let go.

I am grateful to Mark Warren, my editor at Random House, for his attentiveness and advice, and to Zara Houshmand, for her persistence and dedication over the last decade in urging me to write and not retreat into silence. Tina Bennett is a spirited medium—a literary agent who wasn't deterred by this monk's lack of interest in writing something to sell. Cindy

Spiegel encouraged me with the tremendous enthusiasm and sensitivity she expressed toward the book. Alexandra Selby and Elizabeth Campbell spent many weeks transcribing several megabytes of audio recordings.

I am grateful to my Dharma brothers and sisters in Asia and the West, who have often opened their temples and homes for this itinerant monk. My "homelessness" has afforded me many homes, and I feel fortunate to have witnessed that quintessentially human compassion. I am grateful also to my colleagues and friends at MIT as I continue to thrive in this unique culture of inquisitiveness and curiosity, with aspirations to alleviate suffering. Their dedication to what they do inspires me.

I am too young to write a memoir. Priorities in my life may shift but certain aspects of my life will remain rooted in the wisdom of my many past, present, and future teachers. Without their kindness, I would simply be a raft floating in a vast ocean. I am grateful to my students, who continue to teach me many things.

GLOSSARY

•

•

•

Advaita. A nondualism sub-school of the Vedanta school of
  Hinduism.
Aghori. A member of a small group of ascetic Shaiva sadhus.
Ahimsa. Nonviolence or doing no harm, the first precept in
  Buddhism.
Arjuna. A heroic character of the epic *Mahabharata,* who
  was famous for his skill in archery.
Balushahi. A popular pastry of fried dough glazed with
  sugar syrup.
Bhikshu. An ordained Buddhist monk.
Bidi. An inexpensive, leaf-wrapped cigarette.
Bodhi. The "awakened" or enlightened state of a Buddha.
Bodhicitta. A state of mind intent on reaching enlighten-
  ment, motivated purely by altruistic compassion for
  others.
Bodhisattva. An individual confirmed on the path toward
  enlightenment who has not yet become a Buddha. The

meaning evolved over time in different schools and in Mahayana Buddhism emphasized the aspiration to end suffering for all sentient beings.

Chapati. Flatbread of unleavened wheat.

Chuba. The basic garment worn in Tibetan cultures, consisting of an ankle-length woolen robe tied around the waist.

Dacoit. A bandit.

Dharma. A concept in Indian philosophy that has a broad range of meanings depending on context, including natural law, order, and duty. In Buddhism, it popularly signifies the Buddha's teachings and the nature of reality that those teachings point to.

Diksha. A ceremony initiating a layperson into religious life.

Dhoti-kurta. Traditional men's clothing, consisting of an unstitched cloth, wrapped around the waist and legs, and a loose, collarless overshirt.

Drikung Kagyu. A sub-lineage of the Kagyu school of Tibetan Buddhism.

Drona. A character in the *Mahabharata* who is a teacher of martial arts to the heroes of the epic.

Dussehra and **Diwali.** Major Hindu festivals observed as official holidays in India.

Gelug. One of the four major schools of Tibetan Buddhism, popularly known as the Yellow Hat school. A member of the Gelug school is known as a Gelugpa.

Geshe. A higher learning degree in the Tibetan monastic educational system.

Ghat. A series of steps leading down to a river or wharf, used in some places for cremation.

Hanuman. A Hindu god and character in the epic Ramayana, portrayed as a monkey, who represents qualities of strength, self-mastery, and devotion to service.

Kalyanamitra. A spiritual friend, whether teacher or peer, who helps to create the conditions that enable one to mature spiritually.

Khata. A scarf, often made of white silk, that is presented on ceremonial occasions in Tibetan culture.

Khaja. A sweet pastry of deep-fried, layered dough, popular with children.

Kirtan. A musical performance or recitation expressing religious devotion.

Kukri. A distinctive curved knife used by the Ghurkas as both a tool and a weapon.

Kumkum. A red powder made from treated turmeric, used for *tilaka* and religious rituals.

Kurta. A loose, collarless overshirt.

Laddoo. A rich sweet shaped into a small ball.

Lathi. A heavy stick.

Madhyamaka. The Middle Way school of Buddhism popularized by Nagarjuna.

Mridangam. A double-sided drum held horizontally and struck with the fingers or palm of the hand.

Naga. A mythical serpent associated with water.

Nana, nani. Affectionate terms of address for maternal grandparents or other maternal relatives of the same generation.

Prasad. A religious offering of food that is typically consumed by the worshippers after the ritual offering.

Puja. A ritual or ceremony performed as an act of worship.

Rinpoche. "Precious one," a Tibetan title of veneration.

Rimé. A movement in Tibetan Buddhism that was highlighted in the 19th century to counter sectarian tensions while honoring the variety of teachings of different schools.

Rishi. A sage or saint in Hindu tradition.

Sadhu. An ascetic.

Sahib. A title for a person of high rank that was often used in colonial India.

Sakya. One of the four major schools of Tibetan Buddhism.

Samsara. The cycle of death and rebirth, characterized by suffering.

Sannyasi. A renunciant or mendicant.

Sangha. The Buddhist monastic community. In some traditions it refers to all followers of the Buddha, monastic and lay, or to those who have reached a level of realization that gives confidence in the Dharma.

Shaivism. (adjective: Shaivite) One of the major sub-schools of Hinduism dedicated to Shiva.

Shamatha. A form of meditation known as "calm abiding."

Shounin. (Japanese) An honorific title for a monk, priest, or holy person.

Stupa. A reliquary, in some instances referred to as a pagoda.

Sutra. One of a genre of canonical Buddhist texts reserved for the spoken words of the Buddha.

Swami. Literally "Lord," an honorific title used in certain Hindu religious orders.

Tantric. A practitioner of various esoteric traditions.

Thangka. A traditional Tibetan painting on fabric of a religious, often devotional, image.

Theravada. One of the oldest of the extant schools of Buddhism, and now the dominant tradition in Southeast Asia and Sri Lanka.

Thread ceremony. The Upanayana, an elaborate Hindu rite of passage in which a child is initiated into his religious community as an adult and begins his life as a student. It involves the bestowal of a sacred thread that will be worn for life.

Tiffin. A packed lunch or snack.

Tilaka. A mark made with paste or powder, usually on the forehead, with different forms and symbolism in different Hindu traditions.

Tulku. A person whose spiritual accomplishment enables them to deliberately reincarnate, choosing the circumstances of their rebirth in a way that furthers the practice and teaching of Dharma.

Vedanta. One of the six major schools of Hindu philosophy.

Vinaya. The canonical Buddhist texts dealing with the monastic code of conduct.

Zamindar. A title that originated in feudal India for the owner of a large tract of land.

ABOUT THE AUTHORS

THE VENERABLE TENZIN PRIYADARSHI is an innovative thinker, a philosopher, an educator, and a polymath monk. He is the president and CEO of the Dalai Lama Center for Ethics and Transformative Values at the Massachusetts Institute of Technology.

ZARA HOUSHMAND is an Iranian American writer, editor, and literary translator whose work uses empathy to bridge cultural divides. She lives in the mountains of California.